MW01008575

Are You Enough?

Encouragement for the Overwhelmed,
&
Exhausted
Homeschool Mom

by
Roxanne Parks

Are You Enough?
Published by Winter Summit Press
With BeyondYourManuscript.com

Copyright © by Roxanne Parks 2014
All Rights Reserved

All rights reserved. No part of this book may be reproduced or transmitted in any form or by any means, electronic or mechanical, including photocopying and recording, or by any information storage and retrieval system, without permission in writing from the publisher or author.

ISBN – 10: 0615946097
ISBN – 13: 978-0615946092

Cover Art: Diana Smith

Scriptures taken from the Holy Bible, New International Version®. Copyright © 1973, 1978, 1984, 2013 by Biblica INC. TM Used by permission of Zondervan. All rights reserved worldwide. The "NIV" and "New International Version" are registered trademarks in the United States Patent and Trademark Office by Biblica Inc. TM

Published in Association with BeyondYourManuscript.com

What Are People Saying About this Book...?

"As a husband who witnessed the struggles my wife had homeschooling four girls, I can attest to the need for this excellent book by Roxanne Parks. Homeschooling is a calling, but it is very difficult and Roxanne will help all who homeschool by sharing the struggles and victories of her personal journey. I also know her children, and they are a true testament to the benefits of homeschooling. I highly recommend this book."

Joel Manby
CEO, Herschend Family Entertainment
Author of *Love Works* & Father of Four Home Schooled daughters

"Roxanne has been my dearest friend for over 25 years and I was blessed to walk through her homeschool journey with her. I have witnessed how our sovereign God has worked in her life and redeemed the difficult times in the journey. This book has been in Roxanne's heart for a long time and her sole desire is to encourage other moms who may be struggling to stay the course in educating their children and growing them to be the young men and women that they are called to be. What a blessed opportunity to sit at Roxanne's feet and learn from the wisdom that she has gained in her journey."

Shelli Hellinghausen
COO, Perry Office Plus
Board Member for Winter Summit Ministries, Inc.

"What a joy and relief! Roxanne's words are practical, encouraging and scripturally based. She gives flesh and blood to the vaporous dream of successful homeschooling. You will be sighing deeply as you read every page! Thank you, Roxanne!"

Shirley Quine,
Co-founder Cornerstone Curriculum
Homeschool Mother of Nine Children,

"What an encouraging book, a great read for every Christian home schooling mom, whether newbie or veteran! Refreshingly transparent, Roxanne shares how God led and taught her on her home school journey in a way that inspires the reader to know that she, too, can accomplish this great calling. This is a book we wish we'd had when homeschooling our children! "

Tim and Lyndsay Lambert,
President of Texas Home School Coalition
And she is Former Director of Publications for THSC

"This book is a big breath of fresh air! Roxanne Parks takes us with her through her journey as a homeschool mom to 4 now grown children. She is brutally honest in including the ups and downs, the insecurities and the triumphs, the disasters and the victories. The best part of all? She leaves us with HOPE!"

Connie Hughes
Blogger & Publisher at SmockityFrocks.com
Homeschool Mother of Eight Children

"I couldn't stop reading! Roxanne's willingness to share her deepest heart showed me my own needs and reminded me that I am enough! Every homeschool mom needs to read this book."

Lisa Pennington
Author, speaker and blogger at ThePenningtonPoint.com
Homeschool Mother of Nine Children

"With unpretentious transparency, Roxanne Parks relates her journey as a homeschool mom. She reveals the challenges she faced and the lessons she learned from her successes and her failures, offering wisdom, encouragement, and instruction to new and to veteran home educators."

Susan Chrisman
Trustee of Oklahoma Christian Home Educators Consortium
Homeschool Mother of Five Children

"Are You Enough? Speaks right to the heart of every homeschooling mother who has ever asked that question about herself. Roxanne's words are gripping and motivating as she shares her personal homeschool journey, inspiring you to chase after this God-sized dream that He has placed in your heart. Whether you're needing a dose of encouragement as a veteran homeschooling mom or you're testing the waters to see if homeschooling is right for you, this book is a must-read!"

Brandy Ferguson
Blogger and Publisher at TheMarathonMom.com
Homeschool Mother of Eight Boys

Dedication

This book is dedicated to my husband, **Bryan Parks**.
He is the most stable man I know. His patience and
wisdom bless me daily. I believe our greatest season
together lies just before us.
I love you dearly!

Acknowledgements

Matthew, Lauren, David and Jonathan, our children. You guys have been the very greatest teachers in my life. Live your life on purpose and with purpose. I love each of you a bushel and a peck.

The "TEAM" and now dearest of friends: **Laurie Ballweber, Suzanne Baxter, Alison Goodwin, Lisa Harper, Linda Harris, Ingrid Lewis, Kerri Naylor, Andrea Pflughoft & Lisa Rice**. Without your endless support, Winter Summit Ministries, Inc. would not exist. Without your faithful prayers and encouragement, this book would not exist.

Randy Allsbury, my book coach. Without all those crazy inspiring endless accountability sessions... You know! No book! Thanks for your encouraging words at just the right time and doing it over and over again.

Aleta Biddy, my mentor, inspiration, bible study teacher, prayer partner, good friend and most important, an editor "par excellence". I will forever remember just how many red marks improved every page. Thank you for all those hours of sheer detailed work. (Just that. Just that. Just that.)

Shelli Hellinghausen, my life-long dear friend. For the many years we have laughed, cried, and dreamed together, all while raising our precious ones. I am truly grateful for all the things that have purified our friendship.

Jon and Linda Sikes, wonderful friends. Thank you for encouraging us to homeschool and sticking with us all the way. We are still on the same train together just in new horizons.

And to **Dr. Bower, Ralph and Starley Bullard, Marilyn Doerful, Tamara Grady, Margo Hampton, Linda Jones, Janae Nelson, Kathy Piper, Patti Shaw, Peggy Stewart, Grace Whitnah,** and so many friends at **Christian Fellowship Homeschool Co-op.** You have inspired me and walked with me through my homeschool years. I needed your love, encouragement and hugs more than you ever realized.

Table of Contents

Foreword   1

Introduction   5

Chapter 1: The Call to Homeschool   9

Chapter 2: Planning the Vision   23

Chapter 3: Choices, Conventions & Curricula, Oh My   37

Chapter 4: Pressure to Perform   59

Chapter 5: Teaching, Learning & Personality Styles   71

Chapter 6: Wrestling with Guilt, Fear & Inadequacy   81

Chapter 7: Freedom in Discovery   99

Chapter 8: A Fresh Start   117

Chapter 9: Choosing a New Focus   125

Chapter 10: Iron Sharpens Iron   139

Chapter 11: Surrendering All   149

Chapter 12: What You Have **IS** Enough?   161

Foreword

What does one write when asked to "foreword" another author's book? During my career, I have written forewords before, several times in fact. As an avid reader, I have also read a few… That's right. I have read "a few." Yes, having actually read several thousand books during the course of my life so far, I am publicly admitting that I only occasionally read the foreword to a book.

Why? The simple answer is value. Most forewords don't seem to add value to the book itself. I suspect more readers are like me than not. Because your time is valuable, after reading a page or so, if you determine the foreword does not position you to gain greater wisdom from the book itself, don't you skip it and head right to the main course? I do. After all, the foreword is not the book, right?

A foreword is usually written by a person who
1) Is a great admirer of the author.
2) Believes the subject matter is life-changing and is a great admirer of the author.
3) Has his or her own experience in the subject matter,
   and is a great admirer of the author.

Obviously, that "great admirer of the author" thing just has to be there. Curiously, however, in this instance, I have all three of the qualifications listed above. And that is why I believe this foreword can add value to your experience as you read the book it precedes.

Have you ever been overwhelmed by feelings of doubt and fear? As big decisions loom, many people miss what could have been the greatest opportunity in their lives because of those two emotional landmines. Knowing that to be true, allow me to give you a massive infusion of certainty that you have come to the right place for information and perspective about the reality of homeschooling your children.

Yes, it is true. I am a great admirer of Roxanne Parks. Having known Roxanne and her husband Bryan for more than twenty years, my wife Polly and I have had the unique opportunity to watch their four children grow up. The Parks children were very much on our radar as we began having our own. After all, we loved Roxanne and Bryan. As you and I both know, you can fake a lot of things in this life, but you can't fake the kids. And Bryan and Roxanne never had to try.

To this day, the Parks kids—though they are no longer kids—are one of the greatest examples I've ever seen of what you and I have to look forward to as our children learn and grow. First, of course, we must parent our children with the same wisdom and devotion that Roxanne and Bryan have developed over the years. Incredibly, more than two decades of that wisdom has been distilled into the book you now hold in your hands.

I do believe this subject matter is life changing. Now, more than ever, it is imperative that parents connect with their children beyond what today's culture deems adequate. Parenting is quite simply the fulcrum upon which our society tilts. Homeschooling is, of course, nothing if not "advanced parenting." And it is not for the family who has "average" as a target.

In one of my novels, *The Noticer Returns*, the main character is a mysterious old man who helps folks think differently in order to achieve greater results. He says, "If you're doing what everyone else is doing, you're probably doing something wrong. Because everybody is not achieving results you and I would call extraordinary. If you're doing what everyone else is doing, you are merely contributing to the average."

So there it is. Do you want to raise average kids? I didn't think so.

To quickly cover the third reason someone writes a foreword—personal experience—our son Austin is currently being homeschooled. Neither Polly nor I are the mathematical geniuses Bryan and Roxanne must be to have gotten degrees in geology and engineering (whatever that is), but one of the many benefits of the homeschooling experience is the connection to other parents and teachers whose strengths lie in areas where we are not so strong.

I'd like to include a special note here to those of my friends who laughed when I bailed on Austin's math homework in the fourth grade. It is true, I still tremble at the thought of all those numbers, but Austin is in the eighth grade now and currently making A's in algebra. At the eleventh grade level. See? Genetics isn't everything.

I am certain that you will love and appreciate this book as much as I love and appreciate its author. With this volume, Roxanne has created a treasure map for the generational success of your family. Therefore, read it as such. Read it now, read it carefully, and read it with a highlighter!

Andy Andrews
Orange Beach, Alabama

Introduction

Every day, women question their worth and value. Am I cute enough? Smart enough? Skinny enough? Capable enough? Strong enough? Do I have enough of what it takes? Can I stay committed enough to my pursuits? To be certain, homeschooling added layer upon layer of "ARE YOU ENOUGH?" to my journey.

I wrote this book for women who are homeschooling or thinking about homeschooling their children. I want to relay to you that your original ideas and vision for your homeschool will be challenged along the way. What you are doing is counter-cultural and will be under attack. Know that this DIFFICULT journey is so very worth all the effort you have to give. The journey is filled with so many precious moments; however, the fact that you have darling children does NOT mean that it will be an easy job! Your vision may suffer. In fact it may die – perhaps multiple deaths – as you seek to

"What you are doing is counter-cultural and will be under attack. Know that this DIFFICULT journey is so very worth all the effort you have to give."

see that vision through in the future.

My homeschooling journey became my own Joseph story (Genesis 39-41). God had given Joseph a vision but didn't reveal the path to that vision. Joseph suffered many deaths of that vision, but God was always with him. Like Joseph, there were times when I felt as though I had been thrown into a pit, stripped of my perfect little ideas, falsely accused of being a terrible mother and teacher, imprisoned in my own cage of expectations. The homeschooling process forever changed me – changed me in beautiful ways. I don't want to and couldn't go back to being the women I was in my excited but naïve beginnings. The Lord had a greater plan for me and my family than all the plans I had written down –plans for more than I could have ever hoped or imagined. Homeschooling led me to the foot of the cross, and that is the very best place for me to be. In the end, the Lord gave me the very desires of my heart: a freedom to truly trust Him in all things, and a deep peaceful intimacy with Him that I had never known.

Mom, dear sweet mom, I want to deeply encourage you to stay strong in the journey. You have what it takes when you give your two fish and five loaves (John 6) to the great Multiplier to feed your family. Your own children will bear testimony to a life-changing God whose grace and mercy is new every morning. God is wooing you to more. More of Him. More for your family. More rest in His purposes. I am writing to remind you of many things that you know to be true. Ultimately, I want to deeply encourage you, as I have needed such deep encouragement all along the way.

Our four children have all graduated and are now young adults. Hindsight has shown me the absolute value of the homeschool journey. It has forever changed our family, and thus, it will impact future generations. I stand in grateful awe of what God did. Let me tell you the story.

Chapter One

It's All Patty's Fault!

How in the world did I end up homeschooling? Well, it was all Patty's fault. Prior to Patty's decision, homeschooling was never even on my radar! I had heard about those weird people before. Actually, I was very intrigued about the concept but just didn't know anybody who did such a thing, at least not anybody in his or her right mind! Maybe families who lived in the backwoods of some remote place and churned their own butter, but certainly not anyone who lived in a city where you had access to schools. No way would I ever consider such a ludicrous idea.

Then our first child was born! Holding His new creation for our family opened up my thinking to many new ideas. I quickly became a "MOTHER BEAR." You know. Along with

"I was too busy to add another thing. I could barely find my own underwear on a daily basis."

motherhood comes a new, unbelievable, and overwhelming love that would surely help you lift a car off your hurting child. Come on, mother, I know you understand. Falling totally in love with motherhood made me start paying attention to so many more things. It even dusted off the cobwebs of my mind, and I did remember, years before marriage, having attended a conference that promoted homeschooling. Oh my. Those homeschooled students were so obedient, well-dressed, and well-behaved, and they all sang beautifully and in harmony. Yes, I think I might just have to have some of that! Where do I sign up?

As time ticked by and the Lord blessed us with four children in a five-year window, I quickly and quietly swept that homeschool idea under the carpet. I was drowning in all the things that go with three little ones in diapers and four children under the age of six. I was too busy to add another thing. I could barely find my own underwear on a daily basis. Just getting through those days was a real stretch. Deep inside, I was still enamored with the homeschool idea, but there was one thing I knew for sure: I did not have what it takes to be a homeschooling mother! I didn't have the knowledge or the patience, but I did have a long list of flimsy excuses. You know, only THOSE people could do such a thing. I did have a Petroleum Engineering degree from the University of Oklahoma, but in my mind, that didn't qualify me to educate my young, precious, growing, darling, wonderful children. They needed a QUALIFIED teacher. I was not QUALIFIED.

We sent our children to the local Christian school in Midland, Texas, where all my children were born and where we lived at that time. This suited me just fine. I loved the wonderful teachers and was sure that they were QUALIFIED to teach my children. However, one thing still remained – my inner draw to this unique idea of home education.

Since we know that foolishness is bound up in the heart of a child (Proverbs 25:15), it follows that all playgrounds are filled with a bunch of darling fools. In case you haven't noticed, a child needs no instruction in developing a selfish and naively foolish nature. It comes built-in to those darling packages and is called the sin nature. I never taught my children to disobey or lie, but they found a way to do it. I never taught my little ones to be selfish, but they certainly fought over all those things in their life that were "MINE."

So why was I surprised when little Matthew came home one day during his first year at school and asked me the definition of a four-letter word that rhymed with truck? I know that we cannot shield our children from the world in which we live, but I certainly planned to shield them from "too much unnecessary information" as long as possible. This was too big and too foul a word to be discussing with my five-year-old. Another thing I realized was that Matthew could have learned that word in the church Sunday school class as well. I tell you this to let you know it was just another THING that went into my conscience at that time. I think that the sweet Lord was using all these things to draw me back to the idea of homeschooling.

The day finally came when our fourth (and last) child entered kindergarten. For the first time ever, I was looking forward to some peace and quiet around my house during the day! I was going to go to lunch with my girlfriends. I was going to consider joining the YMCA to work out. Now, don't get me wrong: I did enjoy being the mom of four sweet children, but it was definitely time for a break. Dropping our children off at school every day would give me some free time to B R E A T H E.

As the days rolled by with all four finally in school, I realized I deeply missed my children. I would volunteer at their school and watch their teachers enjoy my kids all day long. Their daily absence seemed to draw me right back to the homeschooling idea again. They would come home and tell me all the exciting things they were learning at the hands of their teachers. I wanted to be involved in this beautiful learning process. My kids seemed to be loved by their teachers, but they were still just one – well, four – of many.

We had become close to some friends who were homeschooling their children and loving every minute of it. They would give glowing reports of the benefits of homeschooling. Well, of course, she could do this, but not me, at least not in my mind.

Out of the blue, my eldest son, Matthew (who was nine years old at the time) and his younger sister, Lauren, asked me if I would homeschool them. What!? Absolutely not!!! Not in this lifetime! Not me! I'm not the kind! I'm not smart enough! I will kill my children! I'm not patient enough! What in the world are they thinking? I was blown away with the surprise of this request since I believed that they loved their school and their teachers. I now see their request as another homeschool seed being planted in my heart, so to speak. Now that my children were asking, it was a different question. This was a whole new mental journey for me! The wheels in my mind started churning.

My father had always raised me with a positive mental attitude. Later on in my life, I came to realize that this is simply a way of saying what Philippians 4:8 tells us – to dwell on that which is praiseworthy. At that time, I was attempting to raise my children while looking to the positive. One of our favorite movies was *The Little Engine That Could*. I would always tell them that whenever they were not sure about something, they should imitate that brave little engine. They should say, "I think I can, I think I can." Many times this simple behavior would bring laughter and encouragement amidst a negative moment. But now *I* was in a tough place! I was about to tell my children that I couldn't homeschool. How could I tell them I couldn't when I had taught them to say, " I think I can, I think I can." Instead of not following the message that I was teaching them, I promised that I would at least pray about it. That seem to quiet them momentarily!

Behind closed doors I spoke to my husband about this crazy, lunatic idea that my children had brought up. The idea of us homeschooling! He laughed. What an absurd idea! We laughed together. My husband's first comment to me was, "Well, you can't homeschool our children because you don't even know what year the War of 1812 was fought!" The crazy thing was that I had to ponder that for a second! Did I actually know? His cute but poignant comment actually went right over my head. Amazing! Really? Once I understood his comment, I felt embarrassed, but I knew that this was very clear proof that we were not going to homeschool. Oh my, I didn't even remember that there was a War of 1812! I could not be my children's teacher. I was clearly not smart enough. I was NOT smarter than a fifth-grader. How ridiculous would that be? And then I said, "Well, what do I tell them? We are always teaching them that they can do more than they think they can do."

One of my favorite Bible verses at the time was Philippians 4:13. *I can do all things through Christ who gives me strength.* Just not this. I just couldn't wrap my mind around it at the time. However, my husband and I did

"Don't we need to live on a farm, milk our cows, churn our own butter and make homemade bread to homeschool our kids?"

agree to start praying about it and to keep our minds open. Of course, I could not do all things through Christ if I wasn't even willing to try. I knew that I would not homeschool without Bryan's agreement. It might be a different situation if I were deeply convicted to homeschool, but since I wasn't, I needed him to validate the decision.

As the Lord would have it, it seemed that everyone we asked about homeschooling had a positive opinion. They boasted of the increased amount of family time. They spoke of children testing at above-average grade levels. They highlighted the privilege of being able to hone in on each child's unique gifts rather than a cookie-cutter schooling approach. We became very curious.

Because I thought it would be an overwhelming job, I was going to pull the "submission card" (I Peter 3:5) and agree with Bryan that this was not likely to happen in our house. Besides the simple lack of confidence that his wife was smart enough to homeschool his children, Bryan had a few other big questions: "How do they get high school transcripts?" "How would they ever get admitted to college?" "Don't we need to live on a farm, milk our cows, churn our own butter and make homemade bread to homeschool our kids?" But my inner spirit simply wouldn't let go of this idea. I was drawn to the proposition of the intriguing family journey into home education.

Although all the feedback we received was very positive, it seemed impossible that I actually could do this. What had happened to my faith in *I can do all things through Christ who gives me strength* (Philippians 4:13)? Did I just give the Word of God lip service when it was convenient, or did I really believe it? The icing on the cake that tipped the balance HAPPENED one day when Bryan was given the latest *USA News and World Report.* It contained a positive article about homeschooling. For some reason, that resource was more credible than all the voices we had already heard. The article went on to say that the Ivy League colleges were now recruiting homeschoolers on their campuses. In addition, these homeschooled students brought very desirable character qualities and dimension to their campuses. What? Homeschooled students were actually being recruited to Ivy League college campuses? This idea helped Bryan get over the giant hump of doubt regarding the credibility of this idea.

We took the positive feedback of others, mixed it with the positive article in *USA News and World Report,* and considered it to be God's confirmation that we should homeschool. We were being drawn in. A small spark of excitement started welling deep within me.

A last remaining issue was the looming question of my ability to actually educate our children from home? Did I have what it took? Well, our friend, Jon, asked me, "Roxanne, if you needed to have a job, would you want the job of spending the day with your children, enlightening them and educating them, learning together and discovering together?" He went on to say that I would need to treat it like a job and consider giving it at least 40 hours a week. Well, I didn't want a job. Remember: I was exhausted, and I was ready for a breather! But if I did have to have a job, I believe I would rather have my job be with my children than working behind a desk somewhere else.

Okay, Lord! I'm getting the drift. Since this was such a gargantuan change in my life, I felt compelled, like Gideon, to throw out a "fleece" (Judges 6). I related with Gideon's hesitance and his reminding God of how inadequate he really was. Bryan's agreement to the idea was simply not good enough. My fleece was a prayer to the Lord to confirm his leading by having Bryan offer to teach some classes to help me. I was sure this would not happen because he didn't even want us to homeschool. I was safe with this fleece. But, are we ever really safe? Do I even want to live a life that is safe? No, not really! I want to live a radical, crazy, fun-filled, faith-filled, exhausting, leave-nothing-behind, full, and out-there life!

Yes, you guessed it! Bryan ended up offering to teach Bible and history (of course), and so we began preparing to homeschool the following year.

So, how is this all Patty's fault? Well, Patty is one of my very best friends. She lived directly across the street

"I don't know about you, but it takes me some time to get my mind wrapped around God-sized jobs, and homeschooling, in my mind, was a God-sized job!"

from me, and our families were very close. She is not a homeschooler, but one year she made a wise decision to pull her youngest daughter out of school for a short season in order to develop a rich relationship with her. Her daughter, Heather, was about ten years old at the time, and Patty was attempting to spend extra one-on-one time with her since she was the last child in a very active family. Heather had mentioned to my children that, after school one morning, she and her mom had gone out to lunch and then to the golf course. That was all it took. Homeschool meant golfing and going out to lunch! My children were in! This is what they wanted. Patty had never homeschooled before that year, and she has never homeschooled since. Wow. This must have been another glimpse of God drawing us into His will for our family.

I don't know about you, but it takes me some time to get my mind wrapped around God-sized jobs, and homeschooling, in my mind, was a God-sized job! Sometimes I can tremble at those big jobs, and sometimes I can get so very excited because there's no way I could do it without Him! I had already dealt with the God-sized job issue because, after all, I was a parent, which is a very difficult and humbling job in itself.

One thing I pondered when commencing upon this new homeschool journey was that I was not the first to do this. The wheel had already been created. I did not need to re-create a new wheel, and that gave me comfort. But homeschooling? Really? Me? Would this be a matter of trust? A matter of faith? It appeared that I should not do this journey in my own strength. He started to give me a peace that was past my understanding (Philippians 4:7) and a deep knowing in my mother bear's heart. I should do this! I teetered between that peace and the issue of my own personal competence. Was I capable? Well, I had graduated from elementary school and junior high and high school! I could relearn things right along beside them. We could actually learn together. I didn't have to know everything to start something. That was a bright idea that didn't seem quite so intimidating.

I know there were other educational choices available to us, but all of them involved teachers who could not possibly love my children as much as I did. They certainly could be smarter than me, but not as personally assigned as I was! Did this make me qualified? I would love more! I was more emotionally involved with the outcome of my children's lives. After all, He knit my children together in my womb (Psalm 139). I trusted that He would lead, guide and direct me.

Scripture tells us to teach our sons diligently (Deuteronomy 6:7), to teach them the ways to go when we sit in our house, walk by the way, when we lie down and when we rise up. No matter how insufficient I felt about my ability to homeschool, it was a crystal clear to me that I should be involved in their spiritual and intellectual education of greater things.

As hesitant as my husband had originally been, he was now telling me that I would be great at homeschooling. I believed this to be nothing short of another confirmation by God (considering my husband's original position on the matter). His excitement excited me. We started dreaming about how life might be. No matter what, we knew it would be a great adventure! We wanted our kids to be each other's BEST FRIENDS! We wanted them to be grounded in a genuine faith in Christ and a solid family foundation.

"I hungered to learn more because I had to rise up to the monumental challenge. The mother bear instinct inside me stressed that I could NOT do a bad job at this!"

Basically, I came to my first place of sweet desperation. We were going to actually do this thing, so I needed to find some quick mentors, some much needed information, and I needed it quickly! I hungered to learn more because I had to rise up to the monumental challenge. The mother bear instinct inside me stressed that I could NOT do a bad job at this! No way! The fact that my children's future rested upon my shoulders inspired my preparation as did fervent prayer to my faithful God. I believed that "He didn't always call the equipped, but He always equipped the called." My heart felt called, or drawn, to this incredible, exciting, terrifying journey.

In my desperation to learn more, I clung to a few very important scriptures and promises. I may not have known HOW to homeschool, but I did know WHO could empower me (Philippians 4:13). I knew that His promises were always true. I knew that I should not walk in fear or dread because He would not fail or forsake me (Deuteronomy 31:6). I knew that I should trust in the Lord with all my heart and not lean on my own understanding. I knew that if I acknowledged Him in all things that He would make my path straight (Proverbs 3:5-6). I also knew that no matter how imperfect I was or how apprehensive I felt about homeschooling, He could work all things together for my good since I truly loved Him and wanted His purposes for our family (Romans 8:28). I knew that these truths would become my personal security in my insecure moments.

PRAYER: *Dearest Lord Jesus, thank goodness that You are sovereign and nothing surprises You. Even though I am surprised by the journey that our family is moving toward, I have received your deep peace, which is truly beyond my comprehension. I trust that you will lead, guide and direct me into places unknown. I want your will for our sweet family. Thank you that the seed birthed by Patty that has begun to grow in our home.*
Now, about the vision, Lord... I trust You, Jesus.

Chapter Two

Planning the Vision

In Oklahoma City there is a truly wonderful homeschool-mentoring program. Christian Heritage Academy (CHA) is a "Principle Approach" school that believes in supporting homeschool moms. Their mentorship program is the accountability that many homeschool moms, including myself, needed. It would be impossible for me to say enough nice things about this program during that early season in my homeschool journey. The take-home point here is that I found mentorship and accountability through wise women who had gone before me. This is an important part of beginning to homeschool, and it was a prayer answered!

Through the CHA program, I learned the value of "vision," "mission," and "planning" for the homeschool mom. Scripture is clear about the power of a vision. Proverbs 29:18 says that "where there is no vision, the people perish." My own personal paraphrase of that is "Hey, dummy! If you don't know where you are going, you are not going to get there." Here is another paraphrase: "If you don't have a plan on how to build your house, your marriage, your budget, or your homeschool, then you will likely roam around like the rest of the world and end up with confusion and disappointment." Pray about it. Ask God for a divine download to envision it. Then write it down!

We cannot change what happened in our yesterdays, but we can change how we choose to live our tomorrows.

Don't let the enemy start to put you on any guilt trip this early in the book. I have lived too many years accepting unnecessary guilt for everything. If you have never written anything down about your family goals, marriage goals or homeschool goals, start now.

My husband and I have always been big goal setters. We still set aside one overnighter in the month of January to discuss how our past year measured up in our minds. We then create new goals as we move forward in the coming year. This time together forces much-needed discussion about every area of our lives and marriage. We set our goals in several areas: personal, financial, spiritual, physical, family, marriage and children. Know that we purpose to make this a fun time. We laugh at how we miserably failed at, or even totally forgot, some of our goals. We do not beat ourselves up about the past – that is such an unwise thing to do – but we do look into our future, choosing to

"We cannot change what happened in our yesterdays, but we can change how we choose to live our tomorrows."

move forward in every way.

I love these times together so much that we started smaller versions of these sessions with our children each year when they were younger. It is so wonderful to go back and read some of their precious dreams, goals and hopes for their lives as young'uns. Some of those dreams were simple, with immediate goals, and some, we insisted, were to be five-year, 10-year and future goals for their lives as adults. Our children, to this day, know that their parents believe in the power of asking the Lord to give vision for that which He has called us to do. A planned vision broken down into smaller bite-sized chunks can help to guide your quarterly, weekly and even daily choices.

Back to the CHA program. It taught us about an educational fidelity (1 Corinthians 4:2) which calls us to be faithful in our job to educate our children. Accountability coordinators asked me to pray and discern His vision for homeschooling our children. I needed to write it down. Wow! That was a big thought. I asked them for examples because I didn't know where to start. I knew I wanted something deeply meaningful and clear for our family's education, but I didn't know just how to put that into words. After some coaching, prayer and research, I studied some examples that other families had written. This was a wheel that I didn't need to recreate. CHA had us make everything personal and write it down for our family, a personal philosophy of education.

In order to write a philosophy of education, we went back to *Webster's 1828 Dictionary* to find a definition of "education." I will share this with you below to save you the time and effort of having to look it up yourself. We all need to understand what true education is before we venture off into a journey to educate.

> Education: n. the bringing up, as of a child, instruction; formation of manner. Education comprehends all that series of instruction and discipline which is intended to <u>enlighten</u> the understanding, <u>correct</u> the temper, and <u>form</u> the manner and habits of youth, and <u>fit</u> them for usefulness in their future stations.

To further our understanding of the word education, we looked up the key words as underlined above.

> Enlighten: to give light to; to give clearer views; to illuminate; to instruct; to enable to see or comprehend truth; as, to enlighten the mind or understanding. To illuminate with divine knowledge, or a knowledge of the truth. (Hebrews 6:4)

> Correct: to make right; to rectify; to bring to the standard of truth, justice or propriety; as, to correct manners or principles.

Form: to mold; to model by instruction and discipline; as, to form the mind to virtuous habits by education.

Fit: to prepare, to qualify; as, to fit a student for college.

My ideas were stretched far beyond the predictable reading, writing and arithmetic goals. Studying education in this manner helped me consider the greater value of life-long learning and life purpose. Deuteronomy 6:4-10 calls us to something greater as well.

Deuteronomy 6:4-10 NASB
"Hear, O Israel! The Lord is our God, the Lord is one! You shall love the Lord your God with all your heart and with all your soul and with all your might. These words, which I am commanding you today, shall be on your heart. You shall teach them diligently to your sons and shall talk of them when you sit in your house and when you walk by the way and when you lie down and when you rise up. You shall bind them as a sign on your hand, and they shall be as frontals on your forehead. You shall write them on the doorposts of your house and on your gates. Then it shall come about when the Lord your God brings you into the land which He swore to your fathers, Abraham, Isaac and Jacob, to give you, great and splendid cities which you did not build,"

I challenge you, dear sister and fellow homeschooler, to consider much broader and more eternal considerations than just meeting the academic requirements of your state educational agenda. I share our philosophy, below, just as an example to encourage you. Much of it was written as a compilation of what I had seen others families do that I agreed with and wanted to promote in my own home. Use any parts of it that you believe to be right for your family. I wrote this many years ago, but as I dusted it off recently, I am still impacted by the power of this vision.

"I challenge you, dear sister and fellow homeschooler, to consider much broader and more eternal considerations than just meeting the academic requirements of your state educational agenda."

Parks Philosophy of Education

To ground our children in the Christian faith and to base our education on sound biblical principles

To instill an awareness of the necessity of viewing all of life and learning from a Godly perspective versus the world's perspective

To teach our children the Christian character necessary for Christian self-government

To remind them of God's sure presence in all of life and therefore in the educational process as well

To develop a true yearning in their hearts to know God through His Word and through personal fellowship with Him

To develop an independent love for learning even outside formal schooling

To encourage our children to seek God's wisdom and guidance in all areas of their lives

To prepare our children for future usefulness in their home, in their community, in their state and in their country

To teach them to become independent of their parents and their peers, interdependent with family members and others, and totally dependent on God

A second great instruction I was given at CHA was to study what the Word said about the word PLAN. We learned about an in-depth process of study and revelation called "4-R-ing". It is part of the "Principle Approach" program. The process persuades any participant to Research, Reason, Record and Relate subjects or words from a Biblical perspective. Let me simply summarize the process to encourage you to consider the importance of having a plan to start your journey or, for that matter, your year, your week or your day.

Again, we went to our *Webster's 1828 Dictionary* for the definition:

> **Plan**:
> 1. The <u>representation</u> of any projected work on paper. 2. A <u>scheme</u> devised; a <u>project</u>; the <u>form</u> of something to be done existing in the mind, with the several parts <u>adjusted</u> in <u>idea</u>, <u>expressed</u> in words or committed to writing.

The 4-R-ing process then required that we take the key words (as underlined above) and look each of them up in the dictionary as well. We would sometimes take more key words of the original key words and go deeper and deeper into meaning. After this, we would go to a biblical concordance to see the application of these words in Scripture. We would then pray and reason about the application for us today. 4-R-ing is an in-depth study process that helps someone view a specific word through a biblical lens for a fresh revelation of its application today.

It is certainly not necessary for you to go through this specific 4-Ring process, but I wanted to share with you something I wrote before I ever started to plan out our homeschool journey. Understanding the importance of "planning" and the fact that God is a master planner who has a specific design for all that He has created helped me to really pray through and consider the importance of setting aside time to get my plan-of-action into place. It should not be something that you just throw together; although, I know many that do. I actually failed at some of my planning attempts as well but was always inspired to do better every year.

After my research, I wrote these thoughts on planning:

"The Word of God clearly illustrates the principle of planning. Scripture tells us over and over again that God had "a plan." He designed His creations with specific intention and purpose. There is nothing haphazard about our created world. He is a God of order. It was no accident that the oceans and land were made before the fish and the animals. Nothing about creation just accidentally happened.

The same would hold true for us. God has a plan for every part of His creation. He calls us to follow His plan according to His will. It is a good plan. He created each of us uniquely gifted for a ministry to all believers (Romans 12:6, I Corinthians 12). Therefore, we must seek His wisdom and then plan and act with specific intentions. Things don't just accidentally end up successful. There was a well thought out strategy. There were specifics action steps to follow the plan and move toward the results desired.

Then there is the time and the tenacity required to see the plan through. Fortunately, God doesn't call the equipped but He equips the called through the work of the Holy Spirit.

We must be faithful in prayer to be guided by God in fulfilling His intended ministry in our lives. We must create a plan toward a specific end. We must execute faithfully by His Spirit and ultimately finish the race set before us.

These ideas are very important to a homeschool teacher. It is so important that we are faithful planners of our children's Christian education and lives. Children don't accidentally end up with wisdom and Christian character. Those ideas are seeds that can be intentionally planted in the young souls of our children and when well watered and cared for, can bloom into a beautiful witness for our Lord."

My thinking was very simplistic back then, but sometimes it is the simple things that we can really understand. I love the simple "Jesus loves me this I know for the Bible tells me so." I found it very profitable to consider my plans. They can be simple, but they need to be thought out and defined. What subjects should be taught to each student? What should be your daily and weekly time schedule? What accountabilities should be in place? Then rest in knowing and yielding your plans to His greater plans and purposes.

We also endeavored to have a vision for our marriage and family. The stability of your marriage and your family affects the outcome of your homeschool. Keep first things first! Early in our marriage, we attended a Family Vision Workshop. We learned about leaving a generational heritage through writing down a family mission given by the Lord. My husband and I prayed through this process and wrote the following:

Parks Family Mission: "Life on Purpose"

- We believe that God created each family member unique and with purpose. We will live with eternal perspective in our daily affairs.

- Our family was created and ordained by God as the foundation and priority relationship. We will prioritize and value our family relationships and family fun together.

- We value personal integrity, responsibility, and excellence. We will strive to be self-disciplined, financially independent, generous in giving and respectful of others' property.

- We will strive to know, love, serve, and reflect God. With humility, we will consider others as more important than ourselves.

- We commit to live a positive, joy-filled, encouraging life that is a result of a heart of gratefulness.

- We will teach each family member his/her responsibility to train subsequent generations about his/her Godly heritage and family mission.

Without the encouragement of mentors from CHA, I would not have set very simple, yet powerful, goals. We wanted our kids to become each other's best friends; we wanted more family time together; we wanted to build a strong Christian foundation into our children; we were committed to reading great books out loud, and absolutely, most importantly, we were committed to dancing outside in the rain! This ingenious idea came as the result of all four of our kids being born in the Midland desert of west Texas. Immediately before we started to homeschool, we made a move back to my hometown of Oklahoma City, which was the more fertile home of great thunderstorms and wild weather!

PRAYER: *Oh great God and Abba Father, I tremble at the very vision that you gave us. Let it be true. Let me not grow weary in well doing (Galatians 6:9). I am overwhelmed by the thought of enlightening, correcting, forming and fitting the minds of our own children. I don't want to just teach them but also to train them (Proverbs 22:6) for your purposes alone. I have written things down that I know cannot be achieved without your total grace and guidance. Help me rise up to the task through the indwelling power of your Holy Spirit. Not me, Lord, but You! I trust you, Jesus! P.S. Could You please help me find some curriculum?*

Chapter Three

Choices, Conventions, and Curricula, Oh My!

I was about to go from having four kids in school to homeschooling all four of them in what felt like a moment's notice. Where did I begin to find "the stuff?" What subjects was I supposed to choose? Where was I to begin? Heck, for that matter, what were the subjects that I was supposed to teach at each grade level? All I remember is that you start with the 3Rs: reading, writing and 'rithmetic. But what else? Again, I was feeling completely overwhelmed and totally out of my league. If I couldn't name the subjects a student was supposed to learn, then what was I doing being their teacher? Another wave of doubt came creeping in.

"Wasn't I smarter that a 5th grader? Surely I could research and find out the subjects to teach. I made it through high school, so this should be no big deal!"

Didn't I have a brain? Wasn't I smarter than a 5th grader? Surely I could research and find out the subjects to teach.

I made it through high school, so this should be no big deal! The problem was that I couldn't remember anything that I had previously learned. Making decisions and buying the "stuff" seemed like another overwhelming proposition. I realized that these little things were not little things! This was an early and simple test that I had to pass. What were the subjects that my children needed to learn? Oh my! Really?

If I had not had the help of Christian Heritage Academy, as a mentoring program, I could have searched the Internet for the Oklahoma State school requirements. I got my list from CHA, and I was heading off to the race. But where was I to find the books? Where is the homeschool bookstore? You've got to be kidding me! There is no homeschool bookstore? There is no designated place I can go to find this stuff? No!

I was assigned a wonderful mentor at CHA. The first thing she asked me was what curriculum I using. I quickly responded, "What is curriculum?" She didn't roll her eyes, but I'm sure they were rolling in her head. I was going to be a project.

I later discovered that there are an abundance of curriculum choices. You can be easily overwhelmed, and I was. Not knowing where to start, my mentor said, "Just choose something!" But what something was I going to choose? I prayed for guidance, but I really also needed a choice.

I began asking homeschool moms about their curriculum preferences. Oh my, what a can of worms I opened! Some liked workbooks. Some did not. Some were heavy into reading-type programs. Some liked a "curriculum in a box." Those in-a-box curricula covered all the subjects your student needed in any one given year. Some ladies preferred a hodgepodge of many different choices. Oh my! I was so confused. I simply had to go with my gut instinct regarding what would work for my family. Could I trust my gut instinct? What if I was wrong!? Always asking the Lord to lead, guide and direct me, I was just waiting for the answer. Someone told me that I could get all sorts of choices at a homeschool book fair. I could even get discounted, used book pricing! Okay. I was set and ready to go. Or so I thought!

The fictitious story, below, is really not too far from the truth, just a little exaggerated to make a point.

I was very excited about going to my first homeschool book "fair." I had anticipated it as if I were in my younger years and heading to the local state fair. "Fair" is the important word here. For me and my personality type, that word implied that I was going to have a great time. I looked forward to it – like a little kid who waits for Christmas. I couldn't wait to glean the leftovers from the smart, mature, seasoned veterans who knew all the tricks and had produced perfect kids. I went up to the first table and a perfect mom with perfect teeth and perfect kids convinced me that A Beka was the perfect curriculum. Her kids excelled in every way. I think she said like "A Beka does all the work and you get all the credit." I bought all her used A Beka curriculum. I bought everything she had. I cleaned her out before 9am. I went to the next booth. The mother there told me that she hated A Beka, that her kids didn't learn how to think with A Beka, and that after a year of A Beka and thousands of dollars spent in psychological counseling for both her and her kids, they switched to Bob Jones. Apparently, her kids all graduated Rhodes Scholars and two of them are preparing for senatorial campaigns. I found out I could not return all the A Beka material because it was used and I had bought it for half price, so I bit the bullet and bought the entire Bob Jones curriculum as well. Wouldn't you know, the third booth was pitching Sonlight. By the time I left the book fair, I was a quivering mass of insecure jelly and several thousand dollars in the red.

Okay, okay, that is not a true story, but it does make a point. Each curriculum is unique, and each family is unique. There are no cookie cutter molds!

A dear friend of mine, and an incredible minister to homeschoolers as well as mothers in general, states it this way, "There are no formulas for homeschooling. There are no formulas for life." Really? I just want to put my dollar in the Coke machine, press the Coke button, and get a Coke! That's not too much to ask for. Just what do I need to "put into" the machine of life to get the "Coke" to come out? I just want set-apart, gifted, talented, well-rounded, socialized, God-fearing, intelligent, successful, family-oriented kids. No big request here. So where is that Coke machine? Where is that curriculum? Is this asking too much?

Book fairs ARE great places to learn about books and curricula from people who have actually used them. Sometimes the 27-year-old A Beka salesman has never really used the curriculum to teach his own kids. A book fair is generally a forum for networking and talking with those who have walked the walk with different curriculum and different personalities. It's a great day to go shop with your friends and trade homeschool secrets. Just realize that every woman is different and teaches with her own unique style. Every child is different and learns in a unique style as well.

I came home with a lot of curricula from these book fairs, etc. Some of it I used and loved; some I found didn't work and is sitting on my shelf to this day. Some of it worked great once I worked it, modified it or adapted

"If you have a "failure" of the curriculum or the teacher, but you learn from it, it was never a failure. It was a beautiful learning opportunity."

it. Some worked great when the kids worked it. Some didn't work for me or the kids or the dog. When you have a curriculum failure, it is rarely bad curriculum. There are just so many variables. Did you use it as intended? Did you take into consideration your personality and/or teaching style? Did you apply it properly or consistently? Some people like Coke; some like Dr. Pepper. Personally, I like strawberry lemonade. Realize that it's a preference thing, not a failure thing.

If you try a curriculum that doesn't seem to be effective, try to push through it. If it still isn't working, chunk it and find something you are more comfortable with. Give yourself that freedom. This will teach your kids that plans can change, but decisions don't. If you have a "failure" of the curriculum or the teacher, but you learn from it, it was never a failure. It was a beautiful learning opportunity. As your kids watch you work through these "failures," you will be teaching a greater subject than the subject you were intending to teach. We should teach our children to be lifelong learners so that these so-called failures are just a part of learning to be wiser. As John Maxwell suggests, it is a principle of *Failing Forward* Falling over and over again help a toddler learn to walk. You will catch your stride. No single year is an "end all." You will learn to walk. Be patient and diligent with yourself, your curriculum, and your growing wisdom.

If you embrace the "failure" as an opportunity to learn and become wiser, then isn't it really just a step toward success? Is that what Scripture means when it states that age brings wisdom? Could these failures contribute to my lifelong wisdom? If so, then we should live lives not fearing failure, but fearing that we missed the opportunity to learn from it. A much repeated statement in our homeschool is, "The greatest thing about a mistake is that you get the chance to learn from it!" The goal should be to master a subject, but it doesn't have to happen this month or even this year. Whose race are you in? If something isn't working, give yourself the freedom to change the curriculum, but keep the goal of learning in place.

My advice is to seek wise counsel and then PICK a curriculum. Get started! No matter what you do you, insist that you will succeed. Either the curriculum you choose will prove itself, or, you will succeed by failing forward and becoming wiser. Either way, you win. Let go of that overwhelming feeling and stress of having to pick the perfect curriculum and books! It just drags you down. Believe what Romans 8:28 teaches: "And we know that God causes all things to work together for the good to those who love God, to those who are called according to HIS purpose." Do you love Him and feel called? Do you want your own way? Are you seeking worldly success every step of the way, or are you seeking to be continually transformed by trusting a faithful God? He wants to conform you to His image through every facet of life and homeschooling. Do not fret about choosing a perfect curriculum since you are not the perfect teacher and you don't have the perfect students. Save your energy for other things.

I often have the distinct privilege of mentoring other homeschoolers. I was always eager to listen and learn from others, so I felt it was only fair for me to "pour back in." In one case a lady came to me so broken-hearted, feeling that she was a failure! She went on to explain that her oldest child was a fourth-grader and that they had totally failed to get fourth-grade history correct. She was crying because, in her mind, she was a failure and she believed the lie that surely she could not do this! She was overwhelmed by guilt. I gave her the wise advice I had once received from a mentor myself. I told her that any one school year in any one subject was not a make-it or break-it measuring stick. My mentor had told me to let go of that past year (Philippians 3:13-14). She told me to learn from it and to be extra diligent in that subject for that student the next year. I forgave myself and felt the freedom I needed to move on. I was inspired to get it right the next year. I was learning and failing forward. Why is it that we find great difficulty in giving ourselves any grace? My, oh my! What a great freedom I received from that lesson. My sweet mentee was liberated as well. We must quit beating ourselves up at every turn. I hang myself by my own rope so often. I now think this is just the sly work of the enemy to discourage me. Goodness! Really?

Let me put a word in here about homeschool conventions, since we just talked about homeschool book-fairs. In my humble experience, a homeschool convention is a special time of encouragement, fellowship, and information gathering. Before you go, you must remember the fact that there are no formulas and no cookie-cutter ways of doing things. What is good for the goose just might not be good for the gander. God has uniquely designed your family with unique gifts and purposes. Do NOT ALLOW yourself to be overwhelmed by a homeschool convention. There can be thousands of people attending with hundreds of vendors vying for business. Ask the Lord to lead, guide, and direct you to those things that He has for you. You new homeschooling parents should consider the idea of attending both days of the convention. On the first day, go to just look, learn and listen. After praying yourself to sleep that night, come back the second day and buy sparingly.

The workshops at a convention are powerful tools to answer your questions or to encourage you in a specific area. Usually, the workshop speakers are available for questions and answers outside of the workshop time. Choose wisely. Don't bite off more than you can handle. You want to leave a convention encouraged and with the purchases that will contribute to your educational goals. It is a disservice to yourself to leave a convention overwhelmed and feeling like a failure. That is not the intent. Prayerfully determine to glean that which God will use to equip you.

Most conventions have mentoring booths where you

can learn from mothers who have gone before you. Remember that they are simply volunteers giving you their personal suggestions. They are not the answer to all of your questions, but only one part of the wise counselors you need around you. I love the scripture passages that tell us to seek wise counsel (Proverbs 11:14, 12:15, 13:10, 19:20, 24:6, 27:9). When it comes to any major decision in our family, my husband and I always seek wise counselors. Seeking wise counsel is especially important in places where we are emotionally involved and, therefore, cannot keep a logical bias. I am here to remind you that you are very emotionally involved in the education of your children. The Lord gives guidance through a multitude of counselors/mentors. He also gave me, and is still giving me, grace to learn from my own personal choices and mistakes. This is a life-long lesson as we never grow too old for wisdom from others.

Conventions are often a great place to bring your entire family. Husbands can see a much bigger picture at a convention. Your husband can see a broader group of homeschoolers there. He can gain the feeling that you are not alone in this journey. This is a great place to get your husband "on board." Many conventions even have specific workshops just for men. We have some friends who use the convention as a date weekend each year. This specific husband uses the convention as a means to step into his wife's homeschool world and support her. They choose curriculum together. They attend workshops together. They have lunch together.

My husband has never done that, but I thought it was a great idea. Different strokes for different folks! My husband has no desire to convention with me. It works for us. Don't compare, as you might be disappointed. Either way is the right way for you.

Children are also welcome at most homeschool conventions. This surely gives them the bigger picture as well. If they are old enough, they can sign up for volunteer opportunities, which encourage selfless service and also gives them an opportunities to work with others and meet other teens. There are also several family friendly events.

Conventions are an annual time to recharge your own battery while gathering with like-minded friends. You may even make new friends at a convention. Just remember that each vendor believes in his product and you can't buy them all. Seek wisdom and guidance before you even walk in the door. Promise yourself that you will leave encouraged, and refuse to be overwhelmed.

Okay, once I had started buying curricula, books and supporting materials, I was ready to organize myself in some form or fashion. Through the CHA homeschool mentorship program, I was offered various ways to actually chart out and organize a typical homeschool day. I needed a "compass" or a "map" to guide me.

Before you start to fill out a daily chart, you need to decide the time frame for your school day. What time will my day start? What breaks for fresh air or other activities will I observe? Do I have educational classes outside of our home? When is lunchtime? I put together a daily time chart for each student, covering every subject for that specific year. I computerized this to make replication easier. Remember that these charts are just your compass. We over-achieving moms can strangle ourselves by our very own plans! I did this over and over again. It was exhausting until I decided that I must give myself some grace and just do the best I could do.

Before going any further, you must know that there is rarely a "typical day." Life is ever-changing, and the human condition and emotion changes every day as well. My "CHART" reflected the perfect day. There were no perfect people in my home, but I still needed a standard to reach for. I had to develop the mindset that "all I could do was all I could do." I gave all I could each day and went to bed beautifully exhausted from pouring into my children and being enlightened with them. I had to let go and trust God to help resolve those things that I could not do.

A couple of things that I learned early on were that I liked to start with Bible first and then put math early in the day. I found that my children's minds were sharpest after a good breakfast but faded as the day went on. I also learned that I could group some subjects and teach multiple children at the same time. This was a bit easier when the kids were younger than when they were older. Subjects that may be grouped together are history, bible, read- aloud literature, science etc.

A part of each individual child's chart included the chores that needed to be done that day, as well as any extra-curricular activities like soccer, scouting or music lessons. These daily charts helped to guide us. They were really just big "to do" lists. We felt like we were accomplishing things as we checked off the boxes and proceeded through the day. I was able to make these charts about one month at a time, and each child kept them in his/her own notebook. This also allowed my children to direct themselves during times that I was preoccupied with another children. If they were stuck on a subject and needed my personal attention, they could just temporarily work on something else on their daily chart. You must teach your children to wait until you are free from one thing in order to help them. They need to govern themselves and to keep busy until you are available; otherwise, there will be constant interruptions and nagging that will wear you out.

My charts changed as needed. The very early years of homeschooling young children will look different than my initial charts, and the charts might just be something you want to use personally to keep YOU on track. Likewise, as your students are nearing their final years of high school, these charts will look different.

As your teens become better at self-governance and as they mature into greater independence, you may not even need a chart. We lived with the goal of "those who could govern themselves need not be governed." It was just a goal, but it was difficult to achieve.

You may choose to organize a totally different way. You have many choices, but one thing remains. You must organize yourself and your daily goals in some form or fashion. This book is in no way comprehensive. Most states have homeschool support organizations (like OCHEC.com in Oklahoma) with lots of resources on how to start and set-up your homeschool. I am simply attempting to give you some solutions and encouragement regarding how I handled my daily planning.

Mothers have told me that they hate setting goals (daily or otherwise) because they feel like it sets them up for failure. You must not allow this thinking. You have to have some framework to your school days. Things can be adjusted, but you have to have a foundation from which to start. Remember that we are learning alongside our children each year. We cannot know now what we will learn along the way. This idea demands more flexibility than you might be accustomed. But if you don't learn to be flexible early on, you will certainly get "bent out of shape."

Since laughter is medicine for the soul (Proverbs 17:22), schedule your daily medicine even if you have to put it on the aforementioned chart. A wasted day is a day in which you have not laughed. Since I so desperately had to learn to let go a bit, learning to laugh more helped every day. A stressed-out teacher is not effective. Make a decision to have fun and insist on lots of laughter in your days. Isn't it a sick idea that we would possibly need to SCHEDULE this kind of thing? We all need help reminding ourselves of the importance of some levity in life. I wanted to choose to have happy homeschool days and not be overwhelmed or stressed.

One of my favorite books is *The Traveler's Gift* by Andy Andrews. (See info@andyandrews.com.) Andy is a personal friend of ours. This book was a great read-aloud book for our family. The book shares "Seven Decisions that Determine Personal Success." One part of this book really impacted my determination to include laughter in our days at home. In one chapter of the book, we learn some powerful things from Anne Frank. Anne and her family were Dutch Jews in hiding during the Nazi occupation of Holland in 1943. She shares the fifth gift with the "Traveler." It is her decision to be happy. What a good decision to make! It is both profound and powerful, and I quote:

> *"Today I will choose to be happy. Beginning this very moment, I am a happy person, for I now truly understand the concept of happiness. Few others*

before me have been able to grasp the truth of the physical law that enables one to live happily every day. I know now that happiness is not an emotional phantom floating in and out of my life. Happiness is a choice. Happiness is the end result of certain thoughts and activities, which actually bring about a chemical reaction in my body. This reaction results in a euphoria that, while elusive to some, is totally under my control.

Today I will choose to be happy. I will greet each day with laughter.

Within moments of awakening, I will laugh for seven seconds. Even after such a small period of time, excitement has begun to flow through my bloodstream. I feel different. I am different! I am enthusiastic about the day. I am alert to its possibilities. I am happy!

Laughter is an outward expression of enthusiasm, and I know that enthusiasm is the fuel that moves the world. I laugh throughout the day. I laugh while I am alone, and I laugh in conversation with others. People are drawn to me because I have laughter in my heart. The world belongs to the enthusiastic, for people will follow them anywhere!

Today I will choose to be happy. I will smile at every person I meet.

My smile has become my calling card. It is, after all, the most potent weapon I possess. My smile has the strength to forge bonds, break ice and calm storms. I will use my smile constantly. Because of my smile, the people with whom I come in contact on a daily basis will choose to further my causes and follow my leadership. I will always smile first. That particular display of a good attitude will tell others what I expect in return.

My smile is the key to my emotional makeup. A wise man once said, "I do not sing because I am happy; I am happy because I sing!" When I choose to smile, I become the master of my emotions. Discouragement, despair, frustrations, and fear will always wither when confronted by my smile. The power of who I am is displayed when I smile.

Today I will choose to be happy. I am the possessor of a grateful spirit.

In the past, I have found discouragement in particular situations until I compared the condition of my life to others less fortunate. Just as a fresh breeze cleans smoke from the air, so a grateful spirit removes the cloud of despair. It is impossible for the seeds of depression to take root in a thankful heart.

My God has bestowed upon me many gifts, and for these I will remember to be grateful. Too many times I have offered up prayers of the beggar, always asking for more and forgetting to give thanks. I do not wish to be seen as a greedy child, unappreciative and disrespectful. I am grateful for sight and sound and breath. If ever in my life there is a pouring out of blessings beyond that, then I will be grateful for the miracle of abundance.

I will greet each day with laughter. I will smile at every person I meet. I am the possessor of a grateful spirit.

Today I will choose to be happy."

After reading this part of the book out loud to my kids, we decided to embark upon an experiment. We were going to purposefully add laughter to our days. We could certainly do this for the seven seconds suggested. I put it on our daily chart for a month. A couple of my children were excited about this new experiment, and a couple thought I had lost my rocker. Their teacher had actually lost her marbles! I look back on this simple lesson with great memories. If Anne Frank, a Jew living in wartime Nazi Germany, could mandate and schedule her laughter to keep the daily stresses of life away, then who was I to question such a thing? When I actually looked at the second hand on my watch and told my kids to start laughing, you should have seen a couple of their faces. But as soon as my more sanguine students started ripping into laughter, it drew us all in. Then it became ridiculously funny, and often we went

"Now that all my children are adults, I am convinced that the remembrance of a home full of laughter is what often brings them back."

beyond our seven seconds. I know this may sound as strange as it seems for me to type it, but never underestimate the power of the "medicine" of laughter for challenging moments and days. Now that all my children are adults, I am convinced that the remembrance of a home full of laughter is what often brings them back. Maybe you should come up with your own way to add some levity to your household and to your life. It is good medicine.

On the same charts I scheduled lessons and laughter, I would also list the extracurricular things that we had planned for that school day. This alerted all of us. Throughout our homeschool years, I really tried to include some sort of music class and something of civic or community value. We scheduled piano lessons, scouting and community service projects. Music is a universal language that is very important. I also wanted our children to learn that there was a world out there greater than the world that existed inside the four walls of our home. Some of our greatest times of fellowship and family bonding happened when we were shoulder to shoulder, serving in our community together. This "class" is often left off a homeschool chart, but I found that the things we learned by serving others had a much greater value than the facts we learned in any academic subject. These community service experiences also help children gain a greater perspective on life. As a result, they develop more grateful hearts. There is nothing more powerful for a successful life than a grateful heart. An attitude of gratitude can help us all transform even our worst days. If Anne Frank could transform her difficult days of World War II Jewish persecution and hiding, by her decision to be happy, then I think we all could learn from her.

In all this "planning" of my days, I had to remember that these charts were the GOAL and a compass for our day. I could not allow the plans God had guided me to make to be the very source of total exasperation and discouragement. I had to give our home the grace to just do our very best, even if we fell short of the almighty chart (or whatever measuring stick or planning mechanism you are using). Thank goodness that HIS mercies are new every morning (Lamentations 3:23). If only my mercies could be new every morning, too. Set those goals, but give yourself some freedom when needed. B R E A T H E!

PRAYER: *Oh, Lord, now that I have the stuff, and now that I have the schedule, I begin my faith journey of application. Help each planned day be a reflection of You. I know that I am the first true book that my children ever read. Oftentimes, I am the one whose actions illustrate the truths of Your Word. Establish my footsteps. Make Your face shine upon me (Psalm 119:129-135). Please lighten our days with levity and laughter, as our souls will truly need that medicine. Help me to see divine interruptions as such and to be flexible with our daily schedules. We choose You Lord. We trust you.*

Chapter Four

Pressure to Perform

I have come to realize that behind every face is a story that you do not know. We all wear masks to one degree or another at one time or another. How many times have you been asked, "How are you doing?" and you say, "Fine," regardless of how you really feel. It is just easier. Sometimes we say "fine" right after chaos has broken loose on the home front, or when in the midst of a quarrel with a precious (or not so precious) loved one, or while flirting on the fringes of depression. This certainly happens all the time.

Observe the irony of a stressful Sunday morning: lots of choice words and then screaming and yelling at our kids to get in the car to go to church. After we get through the church doors, when asked how we are doing, we say a quick

"After we get through the church doors, when asked how we are doing, we say a quick 'FINE'. We don't tell someone that we are stressed and mad at all those irritating children in our family."

"FINE." We don't tell someone that we are stressed and mad at all those irritating children in our family. When the time is appropriate, and after asking someone how they are doing, I have learned to often say, "Now tell me how you are really doing." When I am prompted to do this, usually there is a hesitancy followed be a completely different response like, "Do you really want to know?"

Most people don't believe that we genuinely want them to take off the "I am fine" mask. It might take too much time, or we might expose too much information. Therefore, mask wearing is prevalent in our society. Many people live under that "keep up with the Jones'" mentality. Many just don't know how to be transparent, or they don't feel safe being transparent and coming out from behind the mask. In general we are not strong enough or secure enough to tell the real, honest-to-goodness truth. Of course, there are times when sharing is just "too much information." I have had a lot of practice hiding behind the mask. Often, it was simply much easier than the truth. That can work for a while. It can certainly work with acquaintances. Freedom comes in speaking honestly and truthfully to someone. Nowadays, I find it exhausting to display a fake front when I am dying inside. There is a weight we carry around whenever we live behind the mask of "having it all together." Boy, do I know about that. Transparency can bring a real freedom.

As each year of school commenced, I felt an excitement that would be typical of a new beginning, always thinking that this was going to be a super fantastic year. I have to truly admit that there was always this deep, deep "don't want to even admit it" kind of nagging feeling. "What if I am missing something? What if I am doing something wrong? Do I really have what it takes to keep doing this?" You know, just more lies from my "Enemy." I always ignored that feeling and stuffed it somewhere into the recesses of my mind. I would put my mask on and march into my day. Of course, I was unaware of this at the time.

Day after day, I would continue to give all that I knew to impart into educating our children. A very simple and profound truth, which hovered over my days, is that none of us knows what we do not know. Yikes! What a scary thought! Here I am, giving my best, and I don't even know what I don't know. This is a very good reason to keep praying for wisdom on a daily basis. It is also a good reason to stay humble enough to always keep your ears and eyes open. I often pray, asking the Lord to help me see and know more than I currently see and know. I want to see from His eternal perspective. I want spiritual insight and wisdom beyond myself.

To add to my anxiety, the mailman would deliver some quarterly homeschool-type magazine. On the cover, I would see the darling picture of that perfect homeschool family. This would bring to me a deep, nagging feeling of wondering if we could compete with these picture-perfect families on the covers of the magazines. I imagined that their "production and results" of homeschooling far exceeded mine. I would think thoughts like "I am so sure that they are sticking to their school schedule" and "Aren't they so peaceful looking?" and "They even LOOK smart!" I began to feel the need to be like those who were on the cover of the magazine. But since I saw all our flaws, I needed my mask again.

In my very first years of homeschooling, I was very fragile emotionally because I so desperately wanted to be doing everything right. I was not smart enough or strong enough to deal with anything subpar. My children deserved more! I was so busy being busy that if something were missing in our homeschool, it likely went unnoticed. I didn't have time to figure it out. I felt like a hamster running in one of those circular cages. I was running hard, but was I going where I wanted to go? I went to bed beautifully exhausted every night. I gave it my all. I poured my heart and soul into this job of educating my children. If working hard all day made me a good mother and teacher, then I was great!

Thank goodness I had set myself up with the CHA program as an accountability standard. They inspired me. They helped me set goals and plan my year. Then they kept me accountable to my very own stated goals. Oh, if everyone reading this book could have an accountability scenario like this. Well, you can! You will just have to find one or create one on your own. An example would be the accountability of a like-minded friend or homeschool group. There is an inordinate value in being accountable to help you meet your own goals.

Do you really want to know what "birthed" the actual use of those daily accountability charts mentioned in the previous chapter? There is little value in daily charts if you don't actually USE them. Well, at the end of my first nine weeks of homeschooling, I met with my mentor/advisor. She reviewed my list of educational plans. We went subject by subject and checked to see how we were progressing in light of my planning. Seemingly "out of the blue," she asked me how we were doing on spelling words. I looked at her as if she was speaking an unknown language and said, "Ooohhh, spelling words! I knew I was missing something."

This gets back to not only making a daily plan but also the importance of checking your plan. A powerful tool to keep in mind is that we must always "INSPECT WHAT WE EXPECT." Spelling words had slipped through the crack! See, I knew I was going to be a terrible teacher. In my own self-inflicted shame, the lies of the enemy began to flow again. I was totally embarrassed and amazed that I could miss such a seemingly simple thing. But now, I had been caught publicly. The truth was out. Someone out there knew. I was a spelling word failure! My kids were never going to get into college. I had been telling everyone that things were great. Weren't they? Certainly as long as I didn't know what I didn't know, they were great. This began a continuing journey of self-doubt.

Since all four of my kids were below 5th grade at that time, it was not life or death if we missed nine weeks of spelling words, but I learned the valuable lesson of checking my plans against reality. I realized that I could either admit or deny this embarrassing little failure. You know what I noticed? As I had the courage to mention the simple "spelling words failure" story to other homeschool friends in the mentoring program, I discovered that my transparency seemed to be a breath of fresh air. Mouths flew wide open, revealing others with gaps in their imperfect homeschool day. I had dreaded being exposed, but, in truth, I found a grace, freedom, and camaraderie in the revelation of imperfection. What were we all thinking? What masks were revealed? We actually were imperfect teachers teaching imperfect students. It was such a relief to know that I was amidst a group of committed imperfect women just doing their best every day in every way. The last time I checked, there were imperfect teachers in all school systems as well. Why was I expecting myself to be any different? I don't know, but I was. What an ugly and heavy weight to bear!

I was finding a freedom in transparency. The weight of the mask was too great. I started to learn about grace. Little did I know that this would be the beginning of one of life's greatest freedoms – a freedom I would need over and over again. I was finding friends who were delighted to take off their "I've got my act together" masks as well. I was so fortunate to have this experience happen to me in my first year as it would open the door to the reality that no matter how hard I tried, I would never be the perfect homeschool mom, and I might just as well get over that exhausting thought right away! Everyone misses something that she wishes she wouldn't. I needed to learn to give myself a break. This giant learning lesson would be needed more and more throughout my homeschool journey. Over and over again, my kids would need the same grace!

"I started to learn about grace. Little did I know that this would be the beginning of one of life's greatest freedoms – a freedom I would need over and over again."

Do you know how embarrassing it is to learn something and then forget that you know it years later? You have to be reminded again. You may have to relearn the lesson. Well, it happened to me again.

I was sitting in an accountability review time with another homeschool mentor, several years later. She went subject by subject again and asked me how well I was meeting my own goals. When she asked me about 7th grade English, I wanted to slither under my chair. I knew that I couldn't lie to her, but we had really had a pathetic year in that subject with one of my children. As mortified as I was, the embarrassing truth stumbled out of my mouth that I was "7th grade English" failure. I thought that I had learned my lesson with spelling words a few years earlier, but now I was being confronted with the same truth again. I was a failure. Guilt seemed to loom over my days. Another ridiculous mental attack from my enemy. But I bought into it.

Thankfully, my mentor only worked with humans. Since all homeschooling mothers are imperfect and flawed, I was right amidst them. My mentor reminded me that in the course of homeschooling all subjects with four children, I would have some weaker years in any one given subject. It is impossible to do great with every kid, in every subject, every year! I was drowning in the attempt to be so good. I had no idea that the sweet Lord was teaching me another great lesson through my so-called failure.

My mentor gave me grace but also gave me a challenge. She told me to let go of what was past and to set my mind toward having a great English year with this student the following year. I did not get a spanking other than the one that I was giving myself. I found more grace extended from other like-minded women than I could possibly seem to give myself at the time. She was older and wiser and knew what I did not know. She understood that homeschooling was a very difficult journey. She knew that I needed encouragement. I did not need another heap of guilt.

Why is it that we women deal with so very much guilt? Years ago I had a great laugh with a girlfriend, Linda. We were talking about how idyllic our parenting thoughts were BEFORE we were ever parents. We were not going to have "THOSE" kids. Our children would be well-behaved in every way. They would be obedient, clean, respectful, smart, God-fearing and so very talented. Our toddlers would never have boogers running down their noses out in public. How rude and disgusting would that have been?

I didn't become a parent in order to grow up, but parenting has certainly grown me up. Later, I laughed again with Linda after we had been parenting several years. How naïve were we? Nothing stretches you like parenting, but if there were a close second place, it would be homeschooling those kids that you parent. Combine all this together, and you could just have one big guilt trip party. This seems funny to write, but it is a heavy burden to live.

And then there are "those days!" We all have them. I believe that every single parent has those moments that, were they actually caught on a video camera for public display, would cause said parent to shrivel in embarrassment. No one gets it right all the time. You are in good company with the whole imperfect world. Don't beat yourself up over moments that are ugly. This is a condition common to man. It is called sin.

Transparency was never an easy idea for me. You see, my father was a great man. I never recall him saying "I am sorry" or "I love you" while I was young and living at home. His father died when he was nine years old. Being the eldest son in a family of four children, he became the "man" of the house. He also served during WWII. These life events made him a very strong man. He believed that "strength" was exhibited by always being "right." He always believed in doing the "right" thing, and the "right" thing was whatever he thought was "right." I never knew my father to be transparent.

Weakness and tears were not a part of my father's character. Neither was vulnerability. If you ever failed at something, heaven forbid that you would ever admit it. Dust it under the carpet, change the subject, but never show your failure. He considered it a weak thing to do. Not only was I from the "right" family, but also, I was from the "loud" family. The behavior pattern I learned really complicated the weight of masks and failures. Homeschooling just revealed more of my truest self. Oftentimes, I didn't want to know the lady who was sitting in my chair.

Remember that I was NOT homeschooling in order to mature or grow up. Most people quit difficult things. The Scriptures tell us that trials bring about a perfecting of the character (James 1:2-4). The Lord uses trials to sweetly conform us to the image of His character. Well, homeschooling our children was revealing so many personal character issues. My sanguine nature wanted homeschooling to be fun. My choleric nature wanted it to be structured the right way. These goals were being challenged. It was not fun to be exposed, vulnerable, feeling like a failure. A more mature soul had to replace the woman inside. I was confronted with the necessity of becoming transparent with the lady in the mirror and with God. He was refining me and maturing me. I knew deep inside that it was a process I needed to follow. My apparent failures led me back to my global vision, my personal family mission statement. My internal fortitude simply had to increase. I was being transformed daily. My children were worth my transformation, but that didn't make it any easier.

Little did I know that I was just in the early stages of what would become one of my greatest delights in the homeschool journey – growing alongside the children who I was asking and expecting to grow. Hindsight has taught me the value of being strong enough to be vulnerable. On a routine basis, I began ditching the weight of that heavy mask. This continued to bring about more freedom and grace. Ah!

PRAYER: *Oh Lord, I am so grateful that we never have to wear a mask with You (Psalms 139:7-10). I am so grateful that You know me so intimately that You count the number of hairs on my head. Thank You for Your loving patience with me. Help me to be patient with myself and with my children (I Corinthians 13). Give me freedom in the truth. Help me to fail forward right into the sweet palm of Your hands.*
I trust You, Jesus.

Chapter Five

Teaching, Learning and Personality Styles

Have you ever been totally frustrated with your homeschool? Have you ever tried to cram a round peg into a square hole, only to damage everything? Have you ever been totally misunderstood and then confounded by the personality preferences of the people you love the most? I had learned about different types of personalities before I began to homeschool. I just had not taken the time to really study the personalities of my children. You know, you think you know. I am their mother. I get it! I know them. But remember, I was so busy homeschooling. I didn't take time to learn about how we learn. Duh! I was cramming square learning styles and various personality types into all the round and wrong holes, but I didn't know it.

David is an amazingly delightful child. He is such a lover, toucher, and creative soul. He is a feeler more than a doer. He is attentive, and he is a daydreamer. He thinks a day is wasted if someone hasn't noticed the clouds outside, the fly on the wall or the noises you can hear if you will only listen. Forget the books – just run outside and see God's glory everywhere in nature. This type of learner can wreak havoc upon your fit-in-a-box plans. He did not fit into the box. He was designed otherwise. He was a very creative, visual learner. Shame on me for not studying how he learned. But remember, once again, that I didn't know what I didn't know. He needed more freedom to learn as he was created to learn. He was forced to learn in the manner I was teaching at the time. This added so much stress to my homeschool day. It added a burden to our relationship as well. I was cramming my creative child into my mathematical box.

Thank the Lord that I was introduced to right- and left-brain thinking along with various learning styles. I just wished I had learned about this years earlier to save myself so much frustration. In order to become the most effective teacher, acquaint yourself with learning styles by using an assessment test. This knowledge will bless you and relieve your students as they will be able to flourish in their unique, individual ways. You will gain a greater understanding and experience greater result in your teaching efforts. There are many workshops offered on this subject. There is so much research available on the Internet. This was just another thing that I

"I was cramming square learning styles and various personality types into all the round and wrong holes, but I didn't know it."

didn't know that I didn't know.

Here is a quick overview of a few learning styles.

- A visual or spatial learner prefers using pictures, images, and spatial understanding.
- An aural or auditory-musical learner prefers using sound and music.
- A verbal or linguistic learner prefers using words, both in speech and writing.
- A physical or kinesthetic learner prefers using the body, hands, and sense of touch.
- A logical or mathematical learner prefers using logic, reasoning, and systems.
- A social or interpersonal learner prefers to learn in groups or with other people.
- A solitary or intrapersonal learner prefers to work alone and use self-study.

There are many variations on learning styles assessments. God designed each soul with a multi-faceted beauty. No two people are the same. Each of your children have a totally unique God-given design – their own thumbprint, so to speak. When a teacher is unaware of this beautiful fact, she will often miss celebrating a child's uniqueness in exchange for control and stress. What a real shame that I didn't pursue this life-giving information earlier. Every year, continue to ask God for wisdom and understanding of His perfect and unique design for each of your children (Jeremiah 1:5a).

Please do not cram your round pegs into your square holes. Be wise enough to respect the design of the Great Designer when it comes to the unique learning styles and gifts of your precious ones.

Another aspect of this same thinking is the study of personalities. I felt like a light bulb went off in my head when I first became aware of personality assessments. Where had all this information been all my life? Why didn't everyone know about this revolutionary thinking? It totally changed the way I understood people in the world around me. (In my humble opinion, this should be a part of our education system since it will never matter what all we know if we cannot get along with people in an understanding and acceptable way. Just my two cents.)

My first experience learning about personality differences came when I was dating my husband, Bryan. Ann, my dear roommate at the time, gave Bryan and me a personality book to study together as we dated. What a weird idea! She knew what I didn't know. Bryan and I were as opposite as night and day, but I was too in love to realize that our personalities would or could ever be an issue. Thank you, Lord, for Ann! To tell you the truth, studying personalities together was so fun. We would read out loud and laugh at the funny personality stories that Francis Littauer wrote about in her book, *Personality Plus*. We identified many of our own personal strengths and weaknesses in such a light and refreshing way. I cannot tell you what value this was for furthering our relationship.

I am sanguine/choleric. I am an extrovert and always want my world to be social, fun, exciting and full of surprises. I am good at winging it or purely flying by the seat of my pants. I can be up. I can be down. I am an initiator and a confronter. It is very difficult for me to get anywhere on time. I love being in a crowd of friends. I am not very patient and am always talking. I also always want to be in charge and to be right. Remember, I am from the loud family and the right family.

Bryan, on the other hand, is a pure, unadulterated phlegmatic. He is introverted, smart, and stable. He would never fly by the seat of his pants. He doesn't like surprises or being caught off guard. He is not an initiator, and he is not a confronter. He is timely, true, and faithful. He enjoys being one-on-one rather than in a crowd. He is very patient and a good listener. He is neither up nor down. I lovingly refer to him as my "flat liner." He is a true peacemaker, and Mrs. Littauer says that

> *"She wisely told us that the very same things that attracted us to each other while we were dating would be the very things that would irritate us later in our married life."*

every household needs one.

Can you imagine the different ways that these two personalities should be treated and understood? The different ways they may learn most effectively? It was very good for our marriage to understand these things about each other. If you have never studied the personality of your spouse, you are missing a rich blessing that will enable you to strengthen your marriage. God made each of us beautifully unique. After you, He threw away your mold. No one has your unique thumbprint. It behooves you to understand yourself and others better. No one is right, no one is wrong, just different. Learn to appreciate and accept these differences.

We were able to meet Francis Littauer and spend an evening hosting her many years ago when we were a young married couple. She wisely told us that the very same things that attracted us to each other while we were dating would be the very things that would irritate us later in our married life. Boy, oh boy, did she ever nail it? I was glad to remember her admonition later in my marriage as we started to experience additional marital stress due to life issues. We gave each other the freedom to be different from one another. To this day, we often simply agree that we disagree, and then we move on. There are no big fights over things that would predictably be an issue otherwise. We have accepted God's unique design in one another and refuse to have that be a point of contention in our marriage. Our personality differences are not a place of competition but a place of completion. We complement one another by being so different. We have learned to celebrate those differences instead of fight them. We have decided to let one another out of the cage of our expectations.

All of this is to say that if understanding personality types could so enhance our marriage, then I surely would want to understand my children's personality bents as well. There are many personality assessments out there. You can research and find your own "best." Some are more thorough and, therefore, more time consuming. Some are simpler and really fun to do together as a family activity. If you have not done this, I highly recommend it. Life in a family is much easier when you understand these things.

As a side benefit to understanding learning styles and personality types, you will have a greater understanding of what makes other people tick. Since we don't live on an island and we do live in a world of imperfect humans, wisdom with people makes a huge difference. Your people skills will improve. The big pay-off is that you will gain a newfound freedom and understanding of the world around you.

"Our personality differences are not a place of competition but a place of completion."

As the fog of some of my homeschool frustrations began to clear, I could adjust my homeschool day accordingly. Individual personality and learning frustrations had often brought me to the end of my rope. I often felt extremely tired. I have learned that getting to the "end of my rope" can be a very good thing. It usually took me to the foot of the cross, and there is no better place to be. I would cry out for greater wisdom and understanding. I would give my children back to the creator God who had given them to me. I found myself seeking the KNOWER of the answers rather than the answers themselves (Psalm 121). I begged for a wisdom beyond myself. I knew something had to change, or nothing was going to change. What a great idea!

My decision to start each day with some quiet time with the Lord, reading His Word, helped to clear the fog and frustration of homeschooling. He delights in giving fresh revelation (James 1:5) to those who hunger for Him. Why would we want to homeschool in our own strength when we could homeschool in His strength? "I surrender all" become my morning mantra, my waking thought (Psalm 5). It was too exhausting to walk in my fleshly wisdom when He had so much more to give. The Lord is not an adder. He is a multiplier. He multiplies the time that we give to Him. He hears the cries of His people. Cry out for wisdom in clearing your own fog. Ask for a divine download that can bring freedom to some frustrating issues. This will be a work of the indwelling Holy Spirit alone. Yield. Yield. Yield.

PRAYER: *Lord, thank you that we are all fearfully and wonderfully made. Thank you that we all have a unique fingerprint as well as personalities, ways of learning and ways of thinking. I know that You created one body with many parts and ways to serve (1 Corinthians 12). Help me to patiently accept my differences and the differences of my children. Help me to not arrogantly insist on life "MY WAY." Continue to open my eyes, Lord. I want to see as You see. I trust you, Jesus.*

Chapter Six

Wrestling with Guilt, Fear and Inadequacy

As I said in Chapter 4, I grew up with a father who was always right, at least in his own mind. There was always a right way to do things – his way. This caused quite a bit of family tension as the five of us kids were becoming young adults. Whatever I did in life, I yearned to do it the right way. This was an elusive "chasing after the wind." I later learned, after praying for the Lord's wisdom and guidance, that I could only do the best that I could do. That was the right thing for me. But was that going to be enough? My "mother bear" instinct truly despised frequently feeling unsure. Thankfully, most of the time, I walked in a deep peace and confidence, but it was always teetering. Throughout the years I would continue to wonder, deep inside, if I were enough of a teacher to give my children all they needed to walk successfully into their futures.

I wanted to homeschool the right way, whatever that meant! But who knew that distinct right way for my family and our particular four children? As I stated earlier, there is no cookie-cutter mold for homeschooling. Every family is unique and needs to follow their own unique plan. Little did I know that these plans were ever-changing and would require adjustments as needed.

I met a dear friend while our family was attending a homeschool cooperative (co-op). She was as impressive as anyone could be in the academic world. She received her doctorate in the education field. She specialized in teaching school principals how to teach their teachers to teach. Of all the people to meet at a homeschool co-op, she should walk in confidence. She would certainly know how to do it the right way; after all, she was a college professor.

> *"There is no cookie-cutter mold for homeschooling. Every family is unique and needs to follow their own unique plan. Little did I know that these plans were ever-changing and would require adjustments as needed."*

What a surprise it was to me, as I got to know her as a dear friend, when she revealed to me that she dealt with guilt and inadequacy in her homeschool. Really? If she had her doctorate, wasn't she more equipped than I? Even if she had more knowledge, she wasn't free from the burden of guilt. This enlightened me to the idea that all mothers, and especially all homeschool mothers, deal with some level of guilt or failure.

What are we thinking? I actually struggled with feelings that my children would be better off having other women as their homeschool teachers. Other women were much better than I! Is this a crazy thought? God knew what He was doing even if I did not always know what I was doing. I just needed to draw near to Him and trust His work through me.

As unbelievable as it seems, the more I knew, the more I realized that I didn't know. I thought back to my own teenage years when I thought that I knew it all. Just ask most teens if they know more that their mothers. Funny how confident they are and how limited their knowledge is based on the brevity of their life experiences. Scripture teaches us that age brings wisdom (Proverbs 16:31). Life experiences can make us wiser. If that is true, then I think homeschooling expedites our gaining wisdom through new life experiences that come along with the job. This is overwhelming at times.

I now realize that if we wait for all things to be right, we may never do anything. Perfectionistic tendencies often keep us from doing anything. If we all wait for the right time, we may never get married, have a baby, take a much-needed vacation or even write a book. Often times, we miss opportunities while waiting upon the perfect timing. Nothing gets done as we wait for the perfect time to do something. It is an extremely poor excuse for procrastination.

I learned that my perfectionistic tendencies could be blamed on my father, but blaming never brings success. Adam blamed Eve. Eve blamed the snake. But none of the blaming brought success. Blaming is never right, but it is always easy to do. It never leads to real success. When I start blaming, I reveal my insecurities. I am often not even strong enough to admit my own weaknesses. God was continuing to scrape off my sharp edges and mold me.

In addition to perfectionistic tendencies that can drown us, fear can also bring about the heaviness associated with guilt. We must take these fears to the very foot of the cross (2 Timothy 1:7) and leave them there. Fear is so very unproductive. It is a great diversion of the enemy who is always trying to kill, steal, and destroy (John 10:10). The sweet Lord promises us a peace that surpasses all understanding (Philippians 4:6-8). We are more effective in everything we put our hands to when we are at peace. Refuse fear! Stand on His promises when you feel inadequate or afraid. Know that we all have strengths by which to serve others and weaknesses to keep us humble. Do not grow weary in well doing (Galatians 6:9)!

The Scriptures say that whatever you put your hand to, do it with all your might (Colossians 3:23-24). Fear and guilt in your homeschool will take away your might.

Get beyond yourself and walk in His peace. This can only be done when the Holy Spirit is operating through you and you are off your own throne.

I have learned how easily some of us allow guilt to enter our days. Those of us with that perfectionistic tendency also deal very heavily with the guilt of not meeting our own super-sized expectations. We want to be super-mom for our kids. We are hoping to raise super-children. We don't actually say these things, but many of us hope for this deep down inside. Oh my, what an exhausting idea! Free yourself up. Realize that, in your imperfections, you are the perfectly designed mother of your perfectly designed children. God doesn't make mistakes. He was not confused when He gave you your children in the exact order that He gave them to you. Quit trying to control everything!

I am not sure why I choose to allow guilt to hit me on so many levels. Maybe many of you do not respond this way. Here is a short list of some of the guilt trips that the enemy has used to blind me.

1. I am not a good enough mother or wife.
2. I am not a good enough teacher.
3. I am not a good enough organizer.
4. I am not a good enough Christian example.
5. I am not a good enough housekeeper.
6. I am not a good enough neighbor and friend.
7. I am not a good enough homeschooler.

On the other hand, is there some good guilt? Do we sometimes know down deep in our true selves when the feelings of guilt are caused by a lack of discipline and effort? This is the blessing of having a conscience to quicken the spirit to wake up and to rise up and get better! You owe it to yourself to have an excellent homeschool. Your children deserve your best. I thank God for that inner voice that reminds me to rise up and do better. Deep down inside, you know better. It takes effort to do more, but the reward is worth the effort. Step it up, mom! Get better tomorrow. Learn from today. Don't waste the opportunity to mature and improve into your future better self! Wisdom would have you do such things.

Og Mandino wrote *The Twelfth Angel*, a powerful book about a special young boy and a little-league baseball team. It inspires each reader to "get better every day in every way." I happen to love and own the lesson of this quote, for it is a powerful statement that allows me to admit my failures while prodding me to get better. It helps me to forgive myself and others around me who also have the opportunity to get better every day in every way. It gives us all an extension of grace and mercy for our failures, yet it instills within me the desire to grow forward from whatever failure I may have experienced and be better.

I typified myself and my personality as very positive, upbeat, exciting, happy, hard-working, possessing a "can-do" attitude. The heaviness of feelings of guilt, failure, or inadequacy seemed to rob my joy. That was unacceptable to me. Something must be done. The weight of these feelings was too great. A few stories really helped me work through the heaviness that seemed to permeate many of my flesh-filled, embattled days as a homeschool mom.

Please know that I believe that there is "nothing new under the sun" as Ecclesiastes tells us (1:9). Most everything I have ever learned came from somewhere or someone "under the sun." Generations of parents and people inspire the next generation of parents and people. Most everything I've heard that was good for me, I figured might be good for others to hear as well. Wherever I can remember the giver of an idea, I tell you the reference. When I don't refer to someone, I am not sure if the Lord gave it to me or where I specifically learned it. Nothing is new under the sun. Let me retell a great and powerful story.

> *"A buzzard was hungry and looking for food. He roamed over the desert, looking for death and decay to feast upon, as that is what the buzzard eats. He found the death and decay that he was looking for.*
>
> *There was a hummingbird flying over this same desert. The hummingbird was also hungry. He roamed over the same desert, looking for life, flowers, sweetness and nectar to feast upon, as that*

is what the hummingbird eats. He found the flowers, life and nectar that he was looking for.

Two birds. Same desert. One looking for death. One looking for life. They both found what they were looking for. Be mindful of what you are looking for! You may just find it!"

I decided to look for all the life in our homeschool. I began to focus on all the good. I focused on the things we were doing right. Philippians 4:8 reminds us to "let our minds dwell on that which is praiseworthy." This verse is a command. Are we obedient to this powerful, mood-changing verse? Let me illustrate further.

I had searched the world over to find my spouse – the man that I would love and grow with for the rest of my life. Bryan and I got married by choice. No one dragged us down the aisle. No one made me say, "I do." I was delighted at the proposition of our marriage.

When I was dating him, all the things that I loved about him enamored me. I was sure that he was God's gift to me. I chose. While dating and spending some of our evenings studying our personalities, we realized that possible conflicts might arise if we insisted upon NOT accepting each other's God-given tendencies. We talked about areas that we would have to work through as we aged together and the stresses of life came upon us. We learned about each other's strengths and weaknesses. We vowed to love each other for better or for worse, in sickness and in health, in good times and in bad, etc., etc. At that time we never dreamed that trifling little irritations could ever wreak havoc on our marriage. We could not fathom that any kind of perceptual blindness could enter our marriage. We were walking in some kind of bliss that was not tested with time. I felt that same bliss early in my homeschool years with all my educational dreams just waiting to be achieved.

So what happens in a marriage or a homeschool that takes the beautiful lightness and love and hope away? Could part of it be my disobedience in losing focus on that which is praiseworthy? Surely I would never do that. I loved the Lord. But, there came a day, surrounded by the stresses of a young and growing family, financial pressures, homeschooling and extreme busyness that the enemy sneaked into my thoughts like a roaring, crouching lion

"I loved the Lord. But, there came a day, surrounded by the stresses of a young and growing family, financial pressures, homeschooling and extreme busyness that the enemy sneaked into my thoughts like a roaring, crouching lion (I Peter 5:8), waiting to kill, steal, and destroy again."

(I Peter 5:8), waiting to kill, steal, and destroy again. A subtle but deadly change in focus away from things that bring life will surely bring death. Negative thoughts bring death. Negative focus steals, kills, and destroys.

Of course, I was NOT a negative person. I was just an irritated person. I was overwhelmed with all the imperfections and trials of life in our home. I had a little control-freak Hitler who showed up within me sometimes. I was disappointed in everyone, but most of all, I was disappointed in myself for getting to this place! I had lost sight of all that was praiseworthy.

During a certain time in my marriage, I found that I felt so overwhelmed and busy that the enemy got a small foothold on my thinking. I became very irritated about the things that my husband WASN'T doing because I was not focusing on the things that he WAS doing. I became focused on all the things that he WASN'T while not focusing on all the things that he WAS. Why would I do that? When I was dating him, I never even noticed the things that he wasn't. He was more than enough for me at that time. Remember: I chose him? I guess I was focused on what drew me to love him. I didn't stare at his weaknesses. I knew they were there, but we all have weaknesses. We all have strengths.

You know what I was amazed to learn? It was simple, yet oh, so profound! The lady who walked in my shoes was happy when she was dwelling on all the good. She loved Bryan and couldn't wait to marry him. She said "absolutely YES" after she had walked down that aisle. She loved what she loved about him. Maybe she was focusing on that which was praiseworthy?

Then, years later, that same lady changed her focus. She focused on the negative. She focused on what her husband wasn't. She focused on what he wasn't doing. She focused on areas that were irritating. Some of these areas were his weaknesses. She didn't focus on her weaknesses though. She was tired and busy. The truth is that she had changed her focus, and it was sucking the life out of her marriage.

It didn't even matter if any of the negative focus was true. It was still negative. It was not life-giving. She was deeply disobedient in not focusing on that which was praiseworthy, and it was stealing her joy and love for her spouse. Why would she do that?

When she focused on what she loved, she loved him. When she focused on the things she did not love, she didn't even like him and wondered why she had ever chosen to marry him. This is the enemy's subtle ploy.

If you want to breathe life back into your marriage, I want to challenge you as I was challenged. Stop right now and make a list of all the wonderful reasons and character qualities that made you say "YES" to your spouse when you walked down the aisle. Think back and remember moments such as your first kiss and the first "I love you." Get rid of your defensive spirit, take a deep breath, and go back to a love gone by. These things take you back to that woman who delighted in her spouse. Remember! Take time to daydream of those exciting dates when love was fresh and developing. Add more to your list. Now tape that list in the dead center of your bathroom mirror. Read it daily. Remind yourself of that which was praiseworthy. Step into obedience. Refuse to let the enemy rob you of the love that you once shared with your spouse.

As I changed my focus, as I remembered that which was praiseworthy about Bryan, I became thrilled to have him as my spouse again. What a brush with foolishness. What a potentially life-changing impact my disobedience could have had on our home. I remain grateful and humbled by the opportunity to learn this lesson fairly early in my marriage.

Take every thought captive. Your spouse is not your enemy. Understand that you do have an enemy that seeks to destroy your home. He also attempts to destroy your homeschool and your relationship with your children. Learning to love your spouse better each year is the best homeschooling lesson that you could ever exemplify for your students.

Stop right now and make a list of ten things you love about each person living in your household. Ask God to give you the eyes to see. Ask God to reveal more beauty in those around you. Seek goodness. Keep your eyes open for even the smallest bit of goodness shown. Have a praise party in your heart for the little things. Speak of goodness. Let nothing come out of your mouth that does not edify the ears that hear (Colossians 4:6). These actions are an investment in your future. Share the list with those you love. It will be an uplifting exercise for all involved. Refuse to be dragged into discontentment by allowing negative. There are many positive and negative things that life will bring our way. That is not the issue. Focus is the issue. Obedience is the issue. Life is the issue. Promise yourself to work on this. It will be one of the best decisions that you will ever make. Your decision to be obedient, to focus on that which is praiseworthy, will forever change the course of your days. Believe me, it is so worth the effort.

As the Lord would have it, I became the leader of a large cooperative homeschool program. I knew that we all were just women working hard to raise Godly, educated children to the best of our abilities. We needed cooperative help to teach some of the school subjects where we were weak. We were a one-day-a-week program that offered a myriad of classes for all ages.

I knew that I could not lead well if I didn't love, or even like, those whom I was leading. God had given me a sweet co-leader, and we confided in one another that there were some "difficult" women in our group.

So what makes a difficult woman difficult? Have you ever been amidst a large group of mother bears, all of whom are protective of their children? A group of unbridled women could just lead to an ugly catfight. We are proud mommas. We are protective mommas. Don't you tell me about my child's issues. Heaven forbid that I might just tear your head off – if not literally, then in my defensive heart. Did she make a conscious decision to grow up and be difficult? She was one of us. We wanted unity and a family-like atmosphere to undergird the education at the co-op. Are there difficult people in your family like there were at our co-op family? How does one handle that?

My co-leader and I agreed that we could not lead ladies that we did not like. We asked God to blind us to their weaknesses and to open our eyes to their strengths. We refused to dwell on any negative. We looked for the beauty and giftedness in each of our 83 ladies. We celebrated their strengths and put them to work to serve, utilizing their gifts.

Scripture is very clear that God has uniquely gifted each member of His body to serve others within the body. When we identified and celebrated each lady's strengths and unique gifts, she became beautiful right before our eyes. We focused on that which was praiseworthy. Our insistence to only see the positive, lovely, and praiseworthy things resulted in a cooperative program that would function in unity and would encourage all the ladies to focus upon the positive traits of both teachers and students.

I learned that when the leaders of a co-op, or any other group, insist on elevating gifts and the unique beauty in an individual, those they lead usually follow suit. I relearned the truth and importance of believing in people even before they believe in themselves. With enough time, love, and positive encouragement, even the most difficult people will be positively affected.

This change of focus worked in my marriage, it worked at the co-op, and it worked in my homeschool. I want to spend the rest of my life believing the best of others and covering a multitude of sins (I Corinthians 13). We should always give people the benefit of the doubt. This is always a good thing to do. Maybe one day in the future you will find out that they really deserved it and will be glad you did. Or you may find out that they didn't deserve the benefit of the doubt, but you will be glad you gave it to them anyway because it was the right thing to do. This world needs more people focused on that which is praiseworthy than the tearing down of a nation one household at a time with the poison of negativity.

There is life and death in the power of the tongue (Proverbs 18:21). Be wary of the words you permit to crawl out of your mouth. They will indeed affect your marriage, your family, your homeschool, and your future. I am not sure why most of us find it easy to speak before we really think, but the Word of God has a lot to say about this. There are the "slow to speak, quick to listen" scriptures (James 1:19). In Ephesians 4:29 the Word says to "let no unwholesome word proceed from your mouth, but only such a word that is good for edification according to the need of the moment, so that it will give grace to those who hear."

Then there is the simple realization that we were created with two ears and one mouth. Maybe the presumption was that we should listen and learn twice as much as we speak? I have come to realize that this "guarding our tongues" and keeping a "bridle in our mouths" (James 3:1-12) will be a life-long battle. It gets back to the fact that our enemy wants to "steal, kill, and destroy," and so often his tool is the very words that crawl out of our own mouths. This is so very destructive in both your marriage and your homeschool.

I have to constantly stop and give pause to consider my focus and my words. Is my focus on that which is praiseworthy? Are my words a blessing to those around me? Do I speak words that give life or words that bring death? The choice is totally mine. The choice is totally yours. There is no passing the buck or blaming here. Settle this critical life issue by committing to change, improve, grow and mature in this area. It is so worth the time and effort for yourself, those you love, and those around you.

No matter where you designate your homeschool environment (a table in the kitchen, a room in your house, etc.) you always want an intrinsic positive countenance emanating from the teacher – an enthusiasm so to speak – a "Christ-within." If we are coming from a perspective of guilt or inadequacy, then we compromise our ability to shine.

In order to reflect this "Christ-within" or enthusiasm, I found it imperative to live beyond my own human capacity and to allow the sweet, tender, ever-patient Lord to live through me. Beth Moore has produced a Bible Study titled *Living beyond Yourself – Exploring the Fruit of the Spirit.* The Lord did a transforming work in my life through this Bible study. In this study I learned about a freedom that only comes with the emptying of oneself and the filling of the Holy Spirit. It comes with not demanding or deciding the order of your days without an ever-greater yielding to His perfect guiding hand and His divine interruptions. We can be more than we could otherwise be when we have the Holy Spirit living and operating within us. In my homeschool (and in my life in general), I run out of patience and love; the Holy Spirit does not. I am not always sure of how to handle something; the Word tells us to seek after wisdom (Proverbs 4). Instead of just letting go of my plans, I have learned to yield my plans to His greater plans and purposes. This allows a freedom and a flexibility that is imperative to peaceful living.

PRAYER: *Precious Lord, only You are holy! Thank you for carrying the guilt of the world and nailing it to the cross. Help relieve my load of guilt and desperation. I am truly desperate only for You and Your ways. Help me to run the race set before me with an endurance from your Spirit within (Hebrews 12:1-3). Help me to not grow weary and lose heart. Lead me to abide in You alone through Your indwelling Holy Spirit (I John 4:13). Thank you that at the end of my frustrating days, You love me unconditionally. Draw me in, Lord. Transform me by Your faithful love. I need thee every hour. Every hour I need Thee. I trust you, Jesus.*

Chapter Seven

Freedom in Discovery

There are a lot of control freaks out there. I know this, as there is one who often sits in my chair and looks at me in the mirror every day. One assumes a great load to carry when she thinks that she has to be in charge of the world and controlling everything in it. The wise woman knows when TO and when NOT to take control. She also knows when to let go, breathe, and trust that there may be greater things going on than what she had planned –intangible lessons for all to learn. Her children are reading the book of her life in these life-moments. Is she flexible? Is she able to adjust plans without having a fit? Does she yield easily to divine interruptions? Does she have the strength to make quick adjustments and focus on the good of what IS versus what ISN'T happening? Does she have an "un-offendable heart?" If these above questions were on a test, I would flunk!

When we have very young children, we have great control over them, but we

"One assumes a great load to carry when she thinks that she has to be in charge of the world and controlling everything in it."

have absolutely no influence. You get to be in charge of when the diaper is changed, when lunch is served, what they eat, what they wear, who they play with, where they go, what they can watch or even IF they can watch TV. This is a very busy time of life as nothing got into my children's diaper bags unless I put it in there myself. We never got to the park unless I drove my young children there. This time of life fostered an idea, in my mind, that I was in control. It fed the control freak inside me. This was a time in which I actually did have a lot of control of our young family and what happened most days.

As our children get older, we start to lose our ability to have that same level of control, but we gain the ability to have a powerful level of influence. The critical point where these two paths cross varies from individual to individual. Nonetheless, it happens. All my children are now adults. I have no control over their days. I do not choose what they eat, how well they study, where they work, what they read, what they wear, if they read their Bibles, or even who they hang around.

The issue of CONTROL shows up every day in our homeschools. This is another issue with which I constantly wrestled. Many of my homeschooling days were wonderful and delightful. Things seemed to come together like a melodious symphony. Our family seemed to live in a harmony of sorts. Then there were those challenging days that seemed to come out of the blue and made me feel like we were amidst chaos and confusion. If these days happened too often, I became a stressed-out mom and teacher who was not effective. I began questioning my homeschool abilities again. I started feeling like a failure. Did I really think that I could organize many kids, many subjects, many personalities, every day and every way? What in the world was I thinking? I really dislike having very predictable things surprise me.

I came to realize that I spent much of my focus trying to manage my home as well as my homeschool. I was even trying to manage my kids, their thinking, the cleanliness of their rooms, etc. There are times in your young family when a lot of management may truly be needed. But then we all start growing older. God used my friend and mentor, Lynne, to talk to me about being a manager versus being a minister. She challenged my thinking. Was I still running around trying to manage my home? If I didn't manage my home, who would? If I didn't manage my children, who would? At what time does one stop with micromanaging every detail and step into the wisdom of becoming a greater, wiser, minister? Manager versus Minister? Some days you may get to pick how much you can manage; some days you don't. Every day you should be living the overriding call as a minister to those in your home. This idea was hard for me to wrap my mind around. I needed to really seek a wisdom beyond my knowledge: His wisdom. Recognizing this fragile line is important, especially as your children reach those teenage years.

My greater goal was the shaping of Godly character into my children, but there were days that I simply boiled it down to the cleanliness of their rooms and how much we accomplished in the day. My "manager" dominated my ultimate goal of being "minister" in my own home. It took some time for me to really see what was going on. Results seemed to dominate relationship. This new light bulb idea led into my greater learning that rules without relationship leads to rebellion. There were days that I may have insisted on accomplishing some things while my newly hormonal child needed a simple hug, a sensitive heart, or a word of encouragement

As my children became preteens, their independent thinking started showing up. We had actually prayed for them to become independent thinkers, but this developing independence often caught me off guard when it made its appearance. What appeared to be selfishness or a disrespectful attitude may have just been the hormonal start of that "independent thinker" for whom we had prayed. Often, this challenged my control freak down inside. Their newly asserted independent thinking rocked my daily plans. Sometimes I was not smart or wise enough to realize this was an exciting time of transition. I had prayed for children who would grow into capable, competent, independent thinkers. I did not always recognize that my prayers were being answered when we clumsily butted heads throughout those days. This time of transition from control to influence got very muddied by my lack of understanding of these things. Instead of championing the "rise up and have dominion over all the earth" thing that the Lord commanded man to do (which I now can refer to as a very hormonal time), I would often respond in anger that I was being challenged. This is a very real place to seek out the wisdom of the Lord – again.

Emerging young adults and the influence of hormones often left us fighting and me weary. Many of you women got this right. I did not! I confused my maturation taking place in my sons with a confrontational bad attitude. All four of our children were born within a five year and three month window. They were very close in age. When puberty and all its wonderful hormones entered our home, it entered like a whirlwind. I had four teenagers eking hormonal confusion! I wished I were more understanding of this time. I am pretty sure that I was supposed to be the mature one. (Off the record, the real issue may have been my own menopausal hormonal journey that was happening simultaneously). Lord, help us all! Too many hormones under one roof for that stressful season. I pretty much did everything wrong, and that was part of the motivation for me to write this book. Hindsight beckons me to beg for a "do-over," but life does not allow such things. So, back when I needed it, where was all the information that I now know? And who is in charge of information anyway? Why don't we know what we need to know during some of our parenting escapades? Thank goodness that His compassions are new every morning (Lamentations 3:22) and that He can restore what the locusts have eaten (Joel 2:25). I just didn't know how to wisely parent through some of those years. But I sure gave it my 150% best effort. Oh dear, dear friend. Pray for wisdom on a daily basis. This is a must through tumultuous and hormonal days. God wants to take away your stress and exchange it for His peace. Run quickly into His loving arms. Let go, and let God lead!

Little did I know at the time that I needed to start letting go of some of that control and to start focusing on increasing my influence. This was a time for me to really seek the Lord and greater wisdom regarding the fine details of my children's nature. This was a time to start biting my tongue, saying less and praying more. This was a time for me to really talk things out with my husband, who was reading *Wild at Heart* by John Eldredge. One part of the book referred to that age in the life of young, growing, maturing boys in which hormones (therefore confrontation) are on the rise. The author suggested this was a time for mothers to quietly STEP OUT of as many governing things in the life of that teen as possible. It encouraged fathers to STEP IN with more participation and interaction in their sons' lives.

During the teenage years, I worked on transferring as much accountability to my husband as our life would allow. This was not a perfect science. We just did our best to have Dad intentionally speak into our three sons. Every day he, rather than their mother, would speak to them about the things going on in their day. What seemed to them like nagging from me was just a simple question from my husband. There was a respect issue going on here that I was unaware of – It was a MAN to MAN thing. Our sons wanted to be men like their dad and not anything like their mother. Of course they would want to be manly rather than feminine. This is another predictable thing. At this time in a young man's life, the time of increase hormonal development, their mother might make them think of chocolate-chip cookies, Band-Aids, hugs and other loving things. Hormones make a son want to seek an adult male, hopefully your husband, with whom to beat his chest, to chop down a tree, to do manly things with. His mom makes him feel weak and too sweet. He really needs to do more man things. It took me too long to learn this valuable lesson.

Once I began to see the "raising up to have dominion over all the earth hormonal thing" as a season of tender growth for our three young sons, I gladly stepped back, gladly gave up most control, and prayerfully sent them into their dad's man world. Doing so was one of the smartest things we ever did as a couple, but in my thinking, we did not do this soon enough. Thank goodness I believe in failing forward.

There are many things that we moms and dads learn about our children beginning at their births. Then there are those million things that we learn along the way.

One thing I wish I had learned earlier was to really start studying their emerging gifts, preferences, and personality development issues that arise somewhere in the preteen and pre-pubescent days. As I had mentioned before, this is a time that parents need to really study the deeper development of their children. There are many resources on this.

My lack of wisdom caused me to take offense to some of the confrontations that were simply an exertion of my child's newfound ever-maturing thinking. There were many days that I should have taken a deep breath of understanding. I should have been slow to speak at those times and quick to listen (James 1:19). I should have been more mature. However, since my controlled world was being challenged, I would defensively respond, sometimes looking like a five-year-old fighting back. Unbelievable! Surely I was smarter than this! Most often, we find ourselves too busy to seek all the daily wisdom that our sweet Lord is willing to give the hungry-hearted. We need His Holy Spirit operating through us during these harried moments, not us on our own our thrones being defensive. I have always found that my "defensive" self is never my "best" self. It is so very difficult to have an un-offendable heart and to rise above it all in a greater wisdom and maturity. This totally takes a deeper yielding to the Holy Spirit as our flesh natures behave from the sin of self and pride.

Transparency can be a difficult thing. But if the truth were told, every one of us mothers, if recorded at an inopportune time, could host a "Very Embarrassing Mom Moments Show" within the parameters of our own home. No one signs up to be an imperfect parent. No parent signs up to get it wrong. Most parents parent with all of their might. But therein lies the problem. Some days we need wisdom, patience, understanding and love BEYOND our own abilities to give it. We need the grace of the Savior, and our children need His grace offered through the love of their parents. Why do our children think that they sometimes have to work to deserve our grace and love? Thank goodness the Lord's grace and love is a free gift. Only His free gift of grace enables us to love unconditionally, which is the overflow of His indwelling Holy Spirit (I John 4:4, 19).

We only understand what we understand. We only know what we know. Discontentment in a marriage, in a homeschool and in a family, needs to be taken to the foot of the cross. We all deal with feelings of entitlement. So what am I entitled too? There were times when I found myself very tired and without understanding. This was a purifying work of the Lord, but I did not see it as such at the time. I was too busy being busy chasing my ducks. They were not lining up as I had planned. I was losing control. My children's thinking often didn't submit to my schedule each day. I didn't sign up to grow up while my kids were growing up. But that is what needed to happen. I had to go to a place of maturity, surrender, and recommitment where I had never been before. Once again, I had to let go because I was out of answers. I was at the end of my rope. I thought I was in a terrible place. But ladies, hear me on this one! The very end of your rope is the very best place for you to be IF it leads you to the foot of the cross.

During those years when I questioned many things, I can only imagine the Lord writing me this letter.

> *Dear beloved one,*
> *Your children "are a gift from the Lord" (Psalm 127:3). I chose you as their mom. Do not be afraid, as I don't make mistakes. I cannot and "will not fail or forsake you" (Deuteronomy 31:6, 8). I knit those very children inside your womb (Ps 139:13-16). I know the number of hairs on their heads (Luke 12:7, Matthew 10:30). I placed them in My perfect birth order. I entrusted their days to you. It is such a good thing that you have heeded my Word as it is "inspired by Me and profitable for teaching, for reproof, for correction, and for training in righteousness" (2 Timothy 3:16-17) and that you "teach them diligently… when you sit in your house, and when you walk by the way, and when you lie down and when you rise up" (Deuteronomy 6:7, 11). But you need Me to do this incredible job through you, for "My grace is sufficient for you for My power is perfected in your weakness" (2 Corinthians 12:9).*

You need my indwelling Spirit to accomplish all those things that you cannot for Your "Spirit helps our weakness" (Romans 8:26). Are you tired of trying to do it your way yet? Are you weary of your plans not being accomplished to the extent of your dreams and desire? You have a plan, but I have a purpose greater than you plan (Proverbs 19:21). Do you still want it your way, or would you consider yielding to the greater work that I am trying to accomplish through you (John 14:12)? Your "present troubles are small and won't last very long…yet they are produce for us a glory that vastly outweighs them and will last forever" (2 Corinthians 4:17) if you will only turn and allow God to cause all things to work together for the good of those who love God" (Rom 8:28). "If anyone is thirsty, let him come to Me and drink" so that "from his innermost being will flow rivers of living water" (John 7:37-38). I am the answer to your unanswered questions. Do you need a rest beyond what you can seem to get? Then "come to Me" dear "weary and heavy-laden" mom, and "I will give you rest." Unlike yours, "My yoke is easy and My burden is light" (Matthew 11:28-30). Come. Let go of the tight grip that you have around your children and your plans for them. My plans are far greater than your plans (Jeremiah 29:11). "For My thoughts are not your thoughts"…"For My ways are higher than your ways, and My thoughts higher than your thoughts" (Isaiah 55:8-9). You can trust Me more than you can even trust yourself. Let go. Surrender all to me. I am "able to do far more abundantly beyond all that you ask or think, according to My power that works within you" (Ephesians 4:20) Breathe. Rest in ME."

After deciding it was far wiser for me to "let go and let God," I made some new commitments. I decided to go back to the "global" part of my mission statement for homeschooling my children (see chapter 2).

As I looked back on and revisited my original philosophy of education, I realized that I had no great goals of academic loftiness; although, I wanted them to be the best scholars they could be. Many years earlier, my husband and I had prayed about and written goals for our family. We were not seeking conformity with the Jones' but seeking our own standard according to God's guidance. My desperation helped me to reconsider our philosophy. (See Chapter 2.)

"We were not seeking conformity with the Jones' but seeking our own standard according to God's guidance."

These very things that I had written years ago were coming into play in my very own homeschool life experience. I, personally, needed to develop my own faith and character. I needed to be totally dependent on God, to be a life-long learner, to see everything from God's perspective, to yearn for His Word and His ways, to seek His wisdom and guidance. This was in incredible wake-up call. Was I the teacher, or was I really a student?

As I look back, I realize that the Great TEACHER was teaching me more than I could possibly hope to teach my children. He had a very unique plan for me and my family. He was conforming me to His image through the difficulties of the homeschool journey. In my hunger to know more, I begged the Lord to give me new eyes to really see things as He sees them. I did not want to see my children or our homeschool experience through the eyes of myself or others. I did not want to fall into the worldly comparison trap that leads to such discontent. Scripture says, "but when they that measure themselves and compare themselves, they are without understanding" (2 Corinthians 10:12). We never measure up in our own minds. I wanted eyes only for Him and an eternal perspective that could give me some peace.

I wanted to get out of HIS way. I started putting my big-girl panties on and doing harder things like keeping my mouth shout instead of blabbing on and on, things like considering my relationship with my student above the heated issue of the moment. Important things. Yielded things. My priorities switched from getting all the way through our "Homeschool TO DO" list, to never having a day without claiming His glory in the moment. I wanted my very own life to become a book worth reading. I wanted less management and more peace, rest and, wisdom. I wanted our days to be filled with "AWE" over our God and creator. I learned to seek HIM and not seek the answers. "If we seek first His kingdom, all these things will be added unto you" (Matthew 6:33).

I had pondered the thought of HIS plans for my children. Was I good enough or bad enough to thwart His will for my children's lives? I had made myself the all-important center of the universe in my home. What an overwhelming place to live. Could I really be a bad enough mom and teacher that the Lord could not redeem? His Word clearly says that He can make beauty from ashes, bring praise from despair, and joy instead of mourning (Isaiah 6:3). He can restore the years the locusts have eaten (Joel 2:25). Not one of my tears goes unnoticed by the Father (Psalm 56:6). Why was I carrying the weight of the universe and my children's future as if I could be that good or be that bad? This time in my homeschool journey led me to a deeper letting go and ultimate surrender. During this time I started to experience a lightness and freedom that could have only been from the Lord. He was settling my anxious heart and giving me a peace that passed all understanding (Philippians 4:6-7). I learned that if a child failed at something, it wasn't the end of the world. I was not a failure. Maybe God was teaching us about something greater than the failing itself. Was He pointing me toward a deeper understanding of my child's strengths and weaknesses, insecurities, or giftedness? I had been allowing myself to feel defensive and offended at every turn. Praise God that I woke up and challenged myself to have an unoffendable heart. I am still learning about this to the very day of this book's printing. Daily dying to oneself is worth a lifetime of effort.

During this time I made an active choice to be more relaxed. This made a difference in our homeschool days. It is not a choice to do nothing, but a choice to rest in giving my best and then to enjoy a freedom to trust God to fill in my gaps. What a good place for me to be. All of this was caused by my things "getting out of control." Praise God that what the devil means for ill, He can work together for our good (Romans 8:28). I now look back and see all those so-called failures as just stepping stones toward a greater success.

Now that I felt a newfound freedom in our homeschool, I wanted to begin again. I knew that I didn't really get a do-over. But I also know that God can redeem all our mistakes and cause things to work together for good since I love Him and want to live in the center of His will. I rested. I trusted. I crawled off the throne of my life and re-asked Him to stay on it. I never really meant to live out of His will. I was so busy being busy that my SELF slipped into every aspect of our home and my daily plans.

During these days I also learned that I had allowed my children and my homeschooling success to become an idol in my life. I spent more time and energy trying to fix my children, teach my children, and have the best homeschool, than I did in the Word, in prayer or in worship. God was NOT the day-to-day center of my life; although, I knew He was my Savior, and I was certainly hoping that He could save me from the messes that I might be creating. I felt overwhelmed, sometimes because I could never seem to stop the treadmill of my children growing up. I was like a hamster running very fast in my cage, but was I going anywhere that I wanted to be?

If I was the book or the Bible that my children were reading (I never really liked this idea to begin with. It was just another reason for a guilt trip.), then I wanted to reflect more peace, trust, hope, joy, rest, and security in the Lord. I also needed to give myself more grace so that I could give my kids some grace. In my stressed-out moments I didn't even like the woman I had become. I was uniquely created and uniquely gifted, but I was operating way outside of those gifts.

After my desperate "letting go to let God," I felt as if I had another chance in my homeschool world. I wanted to become a student of my students. I wanted to begin to gain a deeper understanding of those He had given us. The Scriptures clearly teach that we are all unique and all uniquely gifted (Romans 12, I Corinthians 12). I felt like I had forced some cookie-cutter plans and ideas onto my family that were wearing all of us out. We were the Parks family. We didn't need to be like any other family. We didn't need to do it like them, to use their curriculum, to have their family rules. The "comparison trap" which I fell into most of the time, was about to kill me.

Boy, have I learned that the grass is NOT greener on the other side of the fence! Our family has experimented with this idea and has proven it to be true over and over again! Most of us have heard that saying before. So why is it that we tend to let our eyes stray over that fence? We should be spending our days seeking HIM and His will and not what others are doing. This great temptation is nothing but a scheme of the enemy to rob, kill, and destroy your peace. Don't buy it!

I asked God to open my eyes to see "that which I could not see." I didn't even know what that was, but I absolutely knew for sure that "I could NOT see that which I could NOT see." I was praying for an enlightenment and revelation as a mother. Instead of looking at my daily school list and what we were or weren't doing right, I began to see individual ideas and gifts in my children. I continued to ask God to
reveal their unique gifts to me. Then I started to build my homeschool days from what God had taught me instead of my daily lesson plans.

Oh, don't be mistaken. I did plan out our academic years with all subjects needed for all children, but I didn't measure our success by A's and B's as much anymore. I measured success more by the quality of our relationships and our level of honoring God with our days and with our words. I wanted my words to be "life-giving," without exception. I had already beaten them down with guilt, obligation, and lack of performance. Boy, am I glad that God doesn't do that to me. Guilt, obligation, and lack of performance – really? His compassion and mercies are new every morning, but I am not sure that mine were. I had hung us all by my expectations. How could my kids feel free to uniquely grow when I already had a plan in place for "how they were supposed to be?" Lord, save us all! I yield my plans to your plans!

PRAYER: *Dearest Lord Jesus, I trust You and pour out my heart to You (Psalm 62:8) for You are my refuge. During this confusing time of hormones and letting go, please lead the way. I am casting all my anxiety on You because I know You love me (I Peter 5:7). I know that Your ways are GOOD and that You work things together for the GOOD. I want Your plans more than my own. Thank You for Your grace as I feel like I am messing things up. I am glad that You can make good out of my messes. I trust You, Jesus....for the little and the big.*

Chapter Eight

Starting Over Again, Again

During that difficult season of discovery, I found a new freedom and the lightening of my load (Matthew 11:28-30). This freedom helped me to begin seeing things with a new perspective. In our home we had an imperfect sinner and very passionate mom trying to homeschool and raise imperfect sinners. None of us were trying to get it wrong. Each day we attempted to do the right thing, so how did I end up with so much stress? Ownership! Simply put, I had ownership of my homeschool, my children, our performance, and our schedules. I was drowning by my own expectations.

When you have streaks of perfectionism running through your soul, you tend to judge others, including yourself. Another characteristic of a perfectionist is that you are never good enough, right enough or smart enough. I also found out that many times I didn't want to do a new thing if I didn't think I could do it well. That is a good trait as long as it doesn't keep you from God's will.

We all know that His plans and His ways are greater than ours but it is very easy to lose track of this idea in the middle of your homeschool busyness. After realizing that my plans had inadvertently gotten in the way of Lord plans, I made a daily choice to intentionally surrender my plans to His and to live with an eternal perspective in mind. I claimed His promise and stood in awe of the fact that He could make good of my messes (Rom 8:28).

During this time I started to think that I might by the "func" right in the middle of my dysfunctional family. Since all families are full of sinners, we are all actually dysfunctional at some level. Our dysfunction is at our core. It is called sin, and we are born with it. No one escapes this trap. Thank goodness we have a redeemer. God sent His son, Jesus, to die for our sins so that we could be new creations. I needed to be a new creation in my homeschool and in my parenting. Thank goodness He sent "the Helper" to help me. His indwelling Holy Spirit was the freedom I needed to breathe! I knew that. Didn't I? But now I really was learning that again. The Spirit within could do so much more than I could ever do on my

> *"When you have streaks of perfectionism running through your soul, you tend to judge others, including yourself. Another characteristic of a perfectionist is that you are never good enough, right enough, smart enough."*

own. It was a matter of yielding once again. This control freak needed a spanking! When would I learn? His ways are BETTER than my ways. YIELD! Be free! The load is too heavy to carry (Matthew 11:28-30).

Homeschooling all kids in all subjects was just what the Doctor ordered to get me to the very end of myself and my proverbial rope. It was a place of yielded rest. I cried out for more of Him and less of me. If only we could spend our lives living totally yielded and in the sweet center of His will. It is this "flesh vs Spirit" battle (Galatians 5:16-18) that keeps us all very humbled. At one point when I was very frustrated with the sinners in my house, I sat down, and the Lord quickly prompted me to make a list of the ERRORS of my ways – not their ways, just a quick list of the questionable areas in my own life. I began to write, and I wrote quickly. My pen could have kept going, but after listing thirty specific areas where I fell short, I decided to stop. It was clear that I had no reason to get frustrated at any of the sinners in my house because, as the mom, I was smack dab in the middle of sin myself. I could so often see the splinter in their eyes but was too busy trying to homeschool and do the right things to actually see the log in my own eye (Matthew 7:3-5).

Here is what I now sweetly refer to as my "DIRTY 30" that flew off my pen all too quickly. I am not proud of these, but they surely keep my feet on the ground.

The Dirty 30

1. *Lose my temper*
2. *Behave selfishly*
3. *Feel depressed and not grateful*
4. *Overeating/Gluttony*
5. *Change my mind*
6. *Change my plans*
7. *Watch an unwholesome movie*
8. *Have a negative tone of voice*
9. *Cast guilt onto others*
10. *Miss my quiet time*
11. *Roll my eyes at others/Belittle them*
12. *Speak defensively*
13. *Judge others quietly*
14. *Talk too much*
15. *Send confusing signals*
16. *Speak a bad word about another*
17. *Spend money frivolously*
18. *Covet things*
19. *Contradict myself*
20. *Self-seeking*
21. *Become impatient or short-tempered*
22. *Quick to presume*
23. *Feel anxious*
24. *Feel superior in any way*
25. *Speak in an unloving manner*
26. *Become overly dramatic*
27. *Become pouty or negative*
28. *Choose laziness*
29. *Criticize*
30. *Become quick to anger*

How could I ever be irritated with my blessings (Psalm 12:7) from the Lord when they were a gift from God to begin with? He made no mistakes when He knit my children into our family. He knew I was going to be their imperfect mom. He knew. I am learning to accept our limitations and to glory in the strengths that He designed into each of us. I learned the enemy often camouflages himself in the irritations of life.

Our home simply needed more grace and mercy and less law and judgment. No one can cast a stone, but I had many in my pocket for those who were not getting things "right." We were all drowning by the laws and schedule of the day. God had mercy on us even when I did not. His quiet love was waiting for me whenever I would plunge into despair or frustration. I cried out for more of Him and less of me (Philippians 3:8-9). As painful as frustration can be, if it leads you to the cross and the freedom given there, it is a beautiful thing indeed. I needed a Holy Spirit download, and I needed it NOW!

Even though there were very many "almost-perfect" homeschooling days in our journey, those days didn't take me to the cross. Those days made me deeply grateful that Patty was my neighbor and that the Lord called me to this wild and crazy journey. I could write many pages of stories of how great homeschooling can be. Most homeschool moms know down deep in their knower that all these good days could not and would not be traded for millions upon millions of dollars. They are priceless. They are worth more than one could hope or imagine, BUT this book is to reveal how I was led to handle the difficult parts of the journey, the deaths of my original homeschool vision.

I really didn't need to cram the world's academic goals down the throats of my children. We were called for something more and different, something our world might not understand. In fact, no one needed to understand that which I was called to do. Deep in my knower, I knew I had to start again with a fresh and new focus. My children might not notice the impending change, but I would know. I would operate in more freedom and less stress. I would study His Word, and I would study my children. I knew that we were each created "on purpose and with purpose." I had to know more of our total life purpose and less of my academic reasons for meeting any state standards. My homeschool teachings had to go way beyond high school into a life mission of living out God's will and purposes for our lives. I needed to see things differently. I needed a lens that only God could give me. I needed to know, be, feel,

> *"My homeschool teachings had to go way beyond high school into a life mission of living out God's will and purposes for our lives."*

and do way beyond that which I was even capable of doing. I needed the Holy Spirit to lead, guide, and direct me into a new territory of greater purpose and freedom.

What did I really want at the end of our homeschool journey? Did I want my students to know Biology? Algebra? History? Absolutely, yes! But if all they gained was knowledge and not the wisdom and character necessary for successful living, then I had missed my mark! I was totally excited deep within. Learning would take on a new dimension that had gotten lost somewhere in the busyness of the years. If trials have a purpose of developing character (James 1:2-4), then the greater things I was learning through my homeschooling journey were certainly a part of that purpose.

PRAYER: *Thank you for convicting me of my dysfunctional ways so that I can be patient with others. Often times, I do the very things that I don't want to do (Romans 7:18-20). Only You are good. Thank you for teaching me more about a compassionate heart. I know we are called for more than just academic results. We want to live out Your designed purpose for each of us! Help us all to learn as you lead, guide, and direct. Keep our eyes open, Lord. We don't want to miss You or Your ways. I know You are with us Lord...every step of the way.*
I trust You, Jesus.

Chapter Nine

Choosing a New Focus

In committing to a new focus and purpose greater than just getting the dad-gum job done, I rededicated myself to seeking a plan greater than my own plan. There was something freeing about recognizing that what is past is past and venturing into a new and brighter tomorrow with the Lord giving a new and fresh fire birthed from the ashes of feeling like a failure. I had a three-pronged focus: redefining relationships, understanding uniqueness in our home, and living each day with a grateful heart. These areas changed my HOW TO and gave me a greater WANT TO.

I paused to consider my relationships in many areas. I purposed to consider a fresh new start in building even greater relationships with my children. I wanted my relationships to rise above my rules. Something I had heard before that I didn't particularly enjoy was

"At the end of our homeschool journey, I wanted deeply bound family relationships more than academic knowledge and excellence."

"You can be right, and you can be lonely." At the end of our homeschool journey, I wanted deeply bound family relationships more than academic knowledge and excellence. I didn't want to get it right and then be lonely because no one in our family actually liked me. Don't get me wrong; I absolutely believe that you can have both. But knowing that the relationship with my children was more important than any knowledge we were cramming into our brains gave me a new compass for the direction of my days.

The first relationship issue that I reckoned with was the idea that my children and my homeschool had grown to become idols in my life. They were the standard by which I gained my worth. This homeschooling journey, and its success, had slipped into a more important position than my marriage and my relationship with God. This was not a truth deep down in my heart but was evident in how I lived out my days. I had traded the priority of my relationships with God and my husband for the priority of my homeschool success. It was all so subtle. Most outsiders would never have known. I barely knew, but I did know. I hated believing that this could even be true. I rationalized, of

> *"The first relationship issue that I reckoned with was the idea that my children and my homeschool had grown to become idols in my life."*

course, that God was more important! Of course my husband was more important. Really?

I had to do some real soul-searching regarding my identity. Was I created to be a wife? A mom? A homeschooler? Was my life measured by these things? Well, then I was indeed a failure on many fronts. Though I was all of these things, more importantly, I was created to bring Him glory, to reflect my Creator (Revelation 4:11). Was I a good mirror of the Designer? Was I missing the mark? This was another place that took me to my knees in a beautiful hunger for truth. I seemed to care more about the world's opinion of our family and success than I did just spending my days trying to walk in and reflect His glory. I had some ugly measuring stick in my mind. I always seemed to be beating myself up inside. Thank goodness I always felt safe falling back into His arms of love, grace, and mercy.

Another area of relationship reckoning that I worked through was the idea of teaching academic knowledge and facts versus core character for future usefulness. I had met a homeschooler that read encyclopedias in his free time. He was a natural vacuum of information. I had met another who made a perfect score on the ACT/SAT test. To be so smart but have no relational success in a world of humans would have been a failure in my eyes. Knowledge is just knowledge. Wisdom is the Godly life-application of that knowledge. If we know everything but cannot relate to our neighbor and successfully live in a world of people, then we have missed great teaching lessons. I, personally, wasn't struggling with too much knowledge. Remember, I didn't know what year the War of 1812 was fought? (Refer to Chapter 1 if necessary.)

At that time, I made sure that in all the teaching of facts and information, there was an even greater teaching and Biblical basis about how to be wise. This took me back to our "Philosophy of Education" again. (See Chapter 2.) I was reminded to use the homeschooling process to teach our children to be fit for usefulness in His kingdom plan and purpose for them. I craved a greater preparedness for life and usefulness, not just the preparedness to get our children into college or to land a great job. The Scriptures teach in many places that wisdom is supreme and that knowledge alone is empty (Proverbs 1-7). This led our family to have a Bible class to study Proverbs and learn about the wise and the foolish. These teachings helped both Bryan and me to constantly re-evaluate our focus. This time also further developed our relationship with our children. During the times that

> *"Everybody is a genius, but if you judge a fish by its ability to climb a tree, it will live its whole life believing that it was stupid."*
> *-Albert Einstein*

they thought a particular class/subject was not going to be pertinent to life, we would remind them of the usefulness of training our minds and preparing for future stations in life. We never get to know the future before it happens, so educational preparation never will hurt you.

Another fresh start came once I reminded myself to study my children's unique design and gifts (I Corinthians 12). "Everybody is a genius, but if you judge a fish by its ability to climb a tree, it will live its whole life believing that it was stupid." Albert Einstein nailed that quote correctly. I often found myself arguing with my "lover-creative child" about math and the likes. He just wanted to hug and notice the clouds while lying in a hammock. His brain did NOT think mathematically. I know that I made him feel "stupid" too many times. I regret that. Therefore, I set out to study my fish! Was I asking them to climb a tree? I asked the Lord to reveal to me His unique gifts in each of my children. I wanted each of them to bloom in their strengths.

I delighted in discovering and learning more about each of our children's uniqueness. I discovered that I had four children with totally different personalities and areas of strengths. I, personally, had one point of view and taught the way I would learn. I needed to broaden the ways I taught. I needed to be all things to all students in my house. This was another God-sized proposition! I spent a lot of time observing the natural tendencies of everyone in my home, even my husband. I had to ask for the Holy Spirit to teach me on a deeper level than I had been learning. The Holy Spirit can reveal things to you that you have not known (John 16:13-15)! He loves to show up and show off when genuinely invited. I felt like I needed wisdom about my children that I had not previously attained. This became a faithful prayer. I needed His eyes to see that which I could not see. I prayed for a deeper connection with my children so that I could help them learn in ways that made sense to them.

What I discovered about my family was that some of us are noticers; some are not. Some of us are initiators; some are not. Some of us are artistic; most are not. Some love groups of people and flying by the seat of their pants; others like reading alone and never being out of their comfort zones. Some of us like surprises; some never want to be surprised. Some of us are fairly concrete and have the ability to understand math and science. Some of us are more free-spirited and vague, causing math to be a foreign and stressful subject. The more I noticed, the more I celebrated the total uniqueness of our family. God had put together a unique group of people in our home. There was no cookie-cutter mold. We each needed the freedom to be different from the others. It was so good to discover strengths and weaknesses and to allow us each to live individually, as created. We all learned that when we focused on the unique strengths of everyone in our home, we were honored to be a part of such a cool family. But when the enemy tempted us to focus on our natural weaknesses, we could actually end up in a fight and not even like each other. This brought everything back to focusing on that which was praiseworthy.

The third area of my new focus was to harness the transforming power of a grateful heart. During my most difficult season of life, we were in a deep and long financial valley that required a move to downsize our house. I had four hormonal teenagers experiencing varying degrees of rebellion. I was in the throes of menopause, and I was the sole caregiver of two aging parents. My dad passed away in my arms after a long journey of decline with congestive heart failure. I absolutely had to live beyond myself during that time. I drank in the Holy Spirit at every opportunity. My plate was so full and overloaded that it was impossible to even consider handling it all in my own strength. That would have been a laughable idea. With the weight of all these things happening simultaneously, I was slipping into depression and overload. Something had to change. It was me.

During this challenging time, my sister-in-law asked me if had read the book *1000 Gifts* by Anne Voskamp. As I was reading the book, I decided to journal all the things I was thankful for. I decided to look for and write down 1000 gifts that the Lord had given me. I did this during the last months of my father's life. Because it was too hard to watch him slowly die, I chose to look for blessings everywhere. I got the chance to serve my dad. I noticed big things and very small things. I was ever looking for the gifts inside each of my days. As I looked for God, I noticed Him everywhere. As I looked for His blessings, I noticed them everywhere. How had I been so blinded? Did I need a depression to lead me to really see? Did my grieving and my load lead me to a better place? This process seemed to help the scales fall off of my eyes. I found delight everywhere as I hungered to see delightful things in those dark days.

The Scriptures promise that our Lord can make all things work together for our good. Through all the difficulties, God was refining my character. Just like the purest of gold, He was purifying me through the heated crucible of my life (Malachi 3:3, Zechariah 13:9). It was a difficult and rich time. I would not want to be the woman I was before He carried me through that particular season. He never did fail or forsake me (Deuteronomy 31:6). Do you need to surrender and let Him carry you through a difficult season? He can handle what you cannot. Take the burdens from your life and give them to HIM (Isaiah 46:4). He is faithful, and He is trustworthy (Psalm 143:8). His plans are truly greater than your plans (Isaiah 55:8). He can do more that you could ever hope or imagine (Ephesians 3:20).

The transformation caused by my grateful heart did not happen the first weeks or months of journaling my thanks and His gifts, but a deep awakening came with choosing a lifestyle of "SEEING," a lifestyle of "LOOKING." It was, and still is to this day, a better remedy than any drug this world could offer. A grateful heart is the best anti-depressant available. I developed a lifestyle of recording blessings. It was a daily discipline. It was life-giving. It was a deep drink of water for a very thirsty heart. After journaling close to 2000 gifts for which I was grateful, I stopped because I was living in a good place. However, as time passed, the enemy sneaked back in and subtly started robbing my joy again. Boy, did I learn a very valuable lesson here: NEVER stop being grateful. I dug my thankfulness journals back out and began recording again. I wrote each day until my joy returned. What a powerful tool we have to fight off the ways of the enemy! This is a life lesson that I will carry with me until I die. It has transformed my days. I will never be the same knowing the transforming power of a grateful heart. Lord, keep me here! I want my eyes WIDE open to your blessings everywhere.

Giving thanks is a matter of obedience for a believer. "In everything give thanks; for this is God's will for you in Christ Jesus" (I Thessalonians 5:18). The Bible does NOT say to give thanks if you are happy or if you like what is going on. It is very clear! In everything! Not just some things, but everything. I found that it was easy to be thankful for the obvious – my children, my husband, a good job, flowers, sunsets, rainbows and the like. I found it was an entirely different matter to be grateful for the hard things of life – the trials and difficult times. It is hard to give thanks for a dying father, or cancer, or an unexpected car accident, or financial difficulties, or a rebellious child. This is where it is difficult to be obedient. We don't only give thanks when it is easy. That would be too simple. Our obedience, trust, and love for God really show up in our decided thanksgiving for the HARD things of life.

During our twelve-year financial valley, I remember thanking God for that time to learn from Him. We had heard that "if your problems are money problems, then you don't really have problems at all." Well, it didn't quite feel that way. However, I did ask Him to teach me what I needed to learn and to do so quickly. It was a purifying time in our lives – a time that we now claim as some of the very sweetest memories of trusting in His provision. Our family nights out became picnics-at-the-park-type things. We would head to the dollar movie theater on 50-cent Tuesdays. That was before the days of the dollar movie rentals. We found a million ways to have fun and not spend money. We laughed a lot. We laughed on purpose!

Giving thanks for many days of teenage rebellion also proved to be difficult. That was not part of my plan, Lord! I homeschooled them thinking that doing so might save us those difficult times. What I learned is that there is no guarantee in parenting or child rearing. I have seen great parents have very rebellious children, and I have seen rebellious parents end up with very God-fearing children. How can this be? Sin is not isolated. It is everywhere. I wanted to sin-proof my home. What a hilarious idea that was, but in my early parenting naiveté, it was a dream. Of course, I knew that we are all sinners and that every parent is raising sinners, but I had hoped to avoid teenage rebellion by making different choices. All that I learned through that difficult time humbled me. It gave me a more compassionate heart. It brought me to the foot of the cross.

Some of the things that the sweet Lord taught me was that He loves my children more that I love them. I was reminded that He is so very trustworthy. I relied on the fact that He knew the truth behind all of their lies. I rested in knowing that none of my tears were cried without His notice (Psalm 56:8). I absolutely stood on His promise to bring about good (Romans 8:28). I hung on to the fact that His promises are always true. I found that there was more power in my prayers for my teenagers than in my words directly to them. I learned that love supersedes guilt or judgment. I learned that a sinner should never call another sinner a sinner. There are never any stones to throw at a rebellious child; we are all rebellious in our sin nature of selfishness. Love is the only answer. I learned, for the umpteenth time, that His mercies are new every morning and that mine should be as well. It was another beautiful and difficult season of refinement. I totally thank God for that season.

"I found that there was more power in my prayers for my teenagers than in my words directly to them."

When you have tasted and seen that the Lord is good and faithful to those who trust in Him and are called according to HIS purpose, you revere those difficult times as a sweet opportunity to draw you into intimacy with your Savior God and Lord. Nothing compares with an intimate relationship with God. It is a high higher than any other high. It can bring a deep and satisfying peace that transcends all understanding (Philippians 4:7). Why wouldn't we want that every single day of our lives? Homeschooling and parenting issues brought me to a greater intimacy with Christ. No matter what life now brings me, no one can take that away.

Years ago, amidst some of these difficult days, I wrote down a thought that has remained in my heart and mind and taped it by our computer. I wrote it as an act of thankfulness during a very difficult time. It says, "Thank you, Lord, for wanting my whole heart and my whole mind and my whole soul so much that you are willing to rip everything away until it leaves me with nothing but a sweet desperation that demands I lay at rest in your arms." Powerful then! Powerful now! Do you need to lie at rest in His arms? Does He need to rip down some of your strongholds through times of refinement and difficulties? Oh, I would pray that you would only see things through the lens of eternity, purpose, and a God who totally adores you enough to draw you near, using whatever measures necessary – even if it is desperation. He never fails; although, our plans just might. Choose a new focus. Use your grateful heart to give you an eternal perspective and the freedom that it brings.

PRAYER: *Thank you, Lord, for being such a patient teacher. I want to be a patient teacher. Lord, bring us deep wisdom from Your warehouse. Help us to seek her with all of our hearts. Thank you for our unique fingerprints and life-prints. Help me learn NOT to jam round pegs into square holes. Free me up to celebrate differences and to be content with the same. Continue to help me see through Your lens. Help me keep my grateful heart a foremost priority. It helps me see You more clearly. Thank you for your endless patience with my learning curve.*
I love You, Lord. I trust You.

Chapter Ten

Iron Sharpens Iron

Feeling inadequate and often overwhelmed by my homeschool, I was led to study and learn valuable things from others. I wanted their iron to sharpen mine. I needed some external inspiration and help from others. It's kind of peculiar that I have come from such a strong "my way or the highway" background, yet I have always wanted someone to mentor or disciple me. Maybe it was that part of my personality that wanted to get things right or do things most efficiently. Maybe it was the part of the Bible that taught us all to seek wise counsel. Early in my 20s, I started to seek women who were successfully living their lives five to ten years ahead of me. Success in a woman that I would desire to emulate meant living for the Lord and honoring Him with my life and choices. I believed that if I had a mentor to give me some great advice, then maybe it would save me a lot of effort trying to figure things out for myself. My mathematic mind

"I believed that if I had a mentor to give me some great advice, then maybe it would save me a lot of effort trying to figure things out for myself."

equated this with efficiency and a "getting further down the road sooner" type thing.

I had also asked my wise ole' Uncle Tom to give me the greatest piece of advice that his 70+ years could give to me as a 23 year old. He told me "some people have to learn everything the hard way. Others (smarter people) watch those people learn everything the hard way, so that they can learn without having to beat their own heads against the wall." Therefore, I quickly became a noticer.

I noticed so many things. I especially liked noticing those people who had good fruit on their trees (Matthew 7:17). I would learn from them and seek short cuts by hoping to avoid doing everything the hardest way first. One of the things I noticed about homeschool students is that generally they had more manners, more of a community heart, and more people skills. This may be attributed to their living lives growing and learning around mature loving adults instead of a large group of same-age peers. Scripture teaches us that foolishness is bound up in the heart of a child. We kept our kids very close to home during their younger years. We didn't need or want them to gain too much information too soon. I could actually feel fairly confident teaching those elementary years. We experienced many unbelievably precious times filled with innocence and naiveté and education.

As our family grew up, we became more involved in educating our children outside of our home. Even though we were very involved in our church, sports, scouts, piano lessons and other social activities, we were very intentional about the boundaries and limits we set for wise living in an unwise world. What we were doing was absolutely counter-cultural. We aspired to live "counter" to so many things in our culture. We desired to be a family set apart. Even though we were totally tempted to live in our bubble, we knew that God had called us to be in the world but not of the world (John 17:14-15), so we prayed about stepping out of the boundary of our home and homeschooling directly with others.

At this time, we sought out greater help from others in the homeschooling community. I was overwhelmed and unsure of my ability to teach upper level classes. I needed help. I needed partnership. I was willing to invest my own talents and gifts to help others as well. I wanted more accountability as well as more like-minded friendships. As always, I was praying for the Lord to lead, guide, and direct me. My homeschool neighbor told me of such an opportunity.

There are definitely times to let others help you! In earlier chapters of this book, I talked about my finding some accountability in the first years through the Christian Heritage Academy Homeschool Program. That program helped me to set higher standards (than I otherwise would have) and also helped me to develop a foundation of teaching through a Biblical lens. I met ladies who inspired me and stretched me. I stayed in that program for five years and loved every minute of it. Later in our homeschool journey, we joined a homeschool cooperative program for families teaching at least one child in the 9th grade or higher. The co-op's purpose was to help mothers teach upper-level students; however, the entire family attended together. Therefore, the co-op include children of all ages, from birth through high school.

I chose to participate in these two programs because I needed more accountability. I needed help from ladies who were smarter than I was. I was smart enough to know that. There are very sharp women out in the homeschool community who are willing to help you in a win-win effort. Besides that, we wanted to meet and grow alongside other families who were on the same journey. We wanted to develop some "community" in our life with like-minded people.

Stepping into a co-op was like stepping into a societal experiment. Mind you, we went to the co-op for upper level academic help. We did not go to the co-op so that mother could grow up. But you know what I found out? There were other families out there who actually did things quite differently than I did, and they believed that they were doing it right as well. But how could that be? Of course, I knew this to be true in theory, but it was a different thing to be confronted with cooperative education, together under the same roof and under a set of co-op policies. Other families had different family behavior codes, different social patterns, different beliefs, and different dynamics. This time became a great classroom for my entire family. I came to call it "Society 101." Intentionally, we chose a co-op program of women who were overtly Christians and wanted Biblical teachings intertwined in the classroom instruction. I loved starting our co-op day in community with others, with a prayer and the Pledge of Allegiance after announcements. Observing such time would not have been allowed in the local school system.

"Society 101" provided opportunities as well as challenges. When you expand your exposure outside the boundaries of your own homeschool thinking and family ways, you learn about many different choices for daily living. We were already very socialized. We knew about all the different ways that people choose to live. We did not object to how the world chose to raise their families; we just wanted to raise ours differently.

Our co-op experience began with 75 other "mother bears" and 200 imperfect children. Each family involved had unique ideas and ways of doing things. I loved the learning curve of locking arms with others for a common and greater good. This had to involve a bit of yielding on the part of all the families because no one thing could be accomplished 75 different ways. This was a lesson in showing a mutual deference to others. Each mom served the co-op in her gifted area.

We served one another so that our families could be served by each other. Each mom served. Kerri taught children math; I taught history. Others taught various classes. Some helped with administration; some cleaned up the lunchroom, etc. My point is that I was ready and grateful to have others help me. I was delighted to step outside our home into a body of Christ (the co-op) that was privileged to exhibit one of the greatest lessons a mom could demonstrate – serving one another. We are commanded to do this Biblically as well (Matthew 23:11; Mark 9:35). We all stretched and served in the co-op. It was a beautiful symphony of the "body of Christ" working together for the greater good.

There was only one little problem: we were cooperating amidst another whole group of sinners. This forced my "Society 101" teaching to my children to be so applicable to real life. I ended up taking the role of leader of this same co-op in my second year of attendance. God totally orchestrated this leadership time to grow me up. I would share with mothers that our co-op (or any other group of homeschoolers working together) was not a place for perfect people because, if it were, then none of us would be welcome there. The co-op was simply an extended community outside of our homes. It was a great place to stretch our scope of instruction to our students. There were teachers at the co-op who didn't teach like I did. This allowed us to learn more about submission to authorities other than parents, whether they agreed with them or not. It was a perfect time to teach our children that they would be working under bosses someday who would also have different personalities and ways of handling things. Some students had different boundaries in their conservative homes. While some parents chose to allow their children to watch TV or certain movies, others limited these choices. We learned that each household has differing opinions about dress, hair length, timeliness, community behaviors, etc. This was a great lesson on the principle of individuality. We all grew in many ways while co-oping together.

When small communities of "mother bears" work intimately together in the lives of their children, many new opportunities arise. If the enemy had his way, there would be vast opportunities to bicker, compare and judge. Educating our children as a group necessitated a much greater maturity, it required more patience, more acceptance, and more deference (Philippians 2:3). Our co-op was full of a wide range of experienced mothers, so it provided the opportunity for a large amount of mentoring and encouragement at all times. As we moms grew in the spiritual unity necessary to co-op in harmony together, our children observed us as life-long learners once again.

The advantage of community taught me so many things that I would not have learned on my own within the walls of our own home. As a leader, I felt a deep desire to really love those whom I led. All mothers lead

145

their children, but God fashions a mega-love in the heart of a mother for this job. Now leading 75 mothers, each possessing different personalities and ways of doing things, I prayed for a wisdom greater than my own. We needed to work co-operatively in peace and harmony. Remembering Philippians 4:8, I was reminded to focus on "that which was praiseworthy" in every mom in our program. I asked the Lord to blind me to their weaknesses and to reveal the beauty, strengths, and gifts that He had designed in each of them. I wanted to see them as He saw them. Like the hummingbird, I was looking for nectar and life in each woman. I wanted to celebrate each of their unique abilities and give them a place to serve with excellence.

I have learned that you cannot out-give the Gift Giver. When we, in the co-op, all served each other in areas of giftedness, it resulted in an indescribable satisfaction that only the Lord can bring. We were created to serve in a body of Christ and to give away that which we have been freely given (Luke 12:48). My entire family grew to love and serve this community. This "Society 101" had become a great classroom. Even though we all had dirty underwear and we were all sinners, it was the next step our family took before my children graduated. We realized that, after graduation from high school, our children would step into an even greater society classroom, that of our fallen world.

As other families in our homeschool community helped us grow and sharpen our irons, we became wiser and more accepting of all of God's unique individuals. I think that every homeschool family, or any family for that matter, should find a like-minded community of people in which to contribute, to learn, to serve, to accept, to celebrate, and to grow alongside in serving Christ together. Maybe it really does take a village. My children learned such valuable things at the feet of other mothers who were teaching them. Those mothers poured Christ's love into my children, all the while educating them in a way that I could not. Praise God for the help of others!

PRAYER: *Dear Lord, thank you so much for community. Thank you for the opportunity to learn from others who work beside us in the accomplishment of a goal. Thank you "for the equipping of the saints for the work of service, to the building up of the body of Christ" (Ephesians 4:11-16). We accomplished so much more together than any one of us could have done on our own. I am grateful for all the lessons learned from co-oping together (I Corinthians 12:13-25). Our family is a small co-operative unit. We work together to live life. Thank you for teaching us about the work of a greater body of Christ to serve one another. We learned such valuable lessons while serving one another.*
To You be all glory! You are so trustworthy.

Chapter Eleven

Surrendering All

The world is full of pride. We all were born with an ugly pride nature (I John 2:16). It is called sin. No matter how much we yearn to be rid of pride, our sin nature is constantly at battle within. My father lost his father when he was nine years old. His mother placed all four of her children into the homes of friends and family for months while she sought an education that would enable her to earn enough money to support her family as a single mom during the Depression years.

After watching this, my father developed a great family pride for his family and simply being together. His mother, my grandmother, learned to type and to do shorthand. Working for our government, she scarcely made enough to feed her children. Because he was the oldest boy, my father felt that he needed to be the man of the house, even at nine years of age. He told me that he learned to NEVER whine because he didn't want to ever let his hard-working mother struggle any more than she already was. Being a single mom of four young children is never easy, but during the Depression, they lived on pennies. At nine years of age, my father would search parking lots for bottle caps to sell to contribute to his family. Then after serving in

WWII at eighteen years of age, he developed another layer of pride, this time in his country.

My dad thought pride was equated with strength. He didn't want his mother or his family to think he was weak as it might add an extra burden upon their family. He also thought that he needed to be right and do the right thing. I don't think that his pride was the result of arrogance; rather, I think it was a "keep-your-head-up-and-never-admit-weakness" thing. His mother needed a strong man in the house even though he was so young.

I am my father's daughter. Pride of country and family is one thing. Pride that looks like selfish arrogance is a whole other issue. Until I became a young adult, I never realized just how much pride was in me. I desperately wanted my father's approval but felt like I was never good enough. In following his footsteps, I would always strive to be right and to do it right. My entire family learned this in our home. After I went off to college, I started to develop a deeper walk with my Lord Jesus. I started to recognize ugly parts of being so proud. It entered my subconscious that there had to be a better way. The Bible has very clear teachings about pride.

"I wanted to be right and to do right in order to show that I was a big girl following in my father's footsteps."

It is an abomination to the Lord (Proverbs 16:5; Proverbs 11). I wanted to walk as the Lord taught but felt trapped in my ways.

Two things that I do not recollect hearing from my father during my younger years were "I love you" and "I am sorry." Never hearing my father say he was wrong or sorry made it very difficult for us children to have our own unique ideas in the household. Most of us children just left for college or other frontiers as soon as we were old enough because of this unyielding nature. We loved him but found it very difficult to have our own opinions while living around him. During my first year at college and my newfound Christian growth, I desired to tell my dad that I loved him. I prayed about the exact time to do this. I remember every detail of this story even now, some forty-odd years later as it was so important and emotional to me at the time. The time had come. I was going to call my father and speak the words "I love you" to him. Someone had to start this conversation that I had hungered for.

At the end of that phone conversation, as I stood behind my dorm room door, I actually got the nerve to speak those words I longed to hear. "I love you, Dad." I cringed and turned away from the phone with barely an ear left close enough to hear a response. I felt awkward but was excited to finally get those words out. I waited. My father said, "Me too." It was disappointing. I wanted to hear "I love you." I realized that those words brought a vulnerability that my father was not strong enough to deal with at that time. His generation was tougher in many ways as he had experienced the Depression and WWII. I was sad but knew that I would try again. I started pondering why in the world this was so very hard to do. Why in the world couldn't we express our love in words? Dad expressed his love in strong provision and guidance in our family.

I realized that our pride made it hard to be vulnerable. This can be a trap. We needed a fresh infusion of the Holy Spirit to transform our thinking. That older generation found it difficult to talk about such things I guess. I wanted freedom – not only freedom to have my own opinion but also to tell someone that I actually loved him or her.

During my college years I wanted to live a more "Christ-centered" life. He knew my struggles with pride. It looked like a "my way or the highway" type of thing. I surrendered to a deep desire to live free of the pride that so ensnared me. I have spent the rest of my life continuing this struggle.

"I continually wondered if I could be good enough or raise good enough kids. I carried this terrible load into my very own family and homeschool."

I have to laugh and tell you that even as my father was growing so weak in those last months of his life, he struggled with his pride and still had to be right. I had finally found my peace with this weakness of his. I would even kid him. In those last months, we were able to discuss previously unmentionable topics. I asked my father who would be right if we had differing opinions on an issue. He laughed and said, "Of course, I would be right because I am your father." We both laughed. I finally was at a place where I could laugh. Because of my security in Christ, I did not need my father's approval on the "rightness" of a thing. God had given me enough strength to understand my father's plight.

Because of this family heritage of pride and needing to do all things right, I seemed to frequently live on a guilt trip. I continually wondered if I could be good enough or raise good enough kids. I carried this terrible load into my very own family and homeschool. If I could pick up some guilt somewhere over something, then I willingly did so. The weight of the desire to always be right left a constant battle in my mind. I say all this to tell you how difficult it must have been to be a child in my home. When my guilt trips got too heavy, I would just throw some guilt trips on my family. Of course, I didn't realize I was doing this at the time.

That is why I am writing to tell you about my own error because of my pride. I gave myself no grace and spent too many days not giving my own children any grace either. I had read that HIS mercies were new every morning, but we just needed to work harder. I exhausted myself so many days with my over-achieving ideas. We spent a lot of time reaching for standards beyond possibility, which always caused a subtle feeling of failure, even though I never called it such at the time. After many years, this failure feeling showed up in sometimes-ugly ways. I didn't always like the lady who sat in my chair. She was never good enough – not even for her children or her family. Pride leading to guilt is a bitter root. I continue to pray for freedom from its chains! Writing this might be my "Therapy 101," huh?

Actually, let me insert here that I believe every momma needs her therapy. Find it, girls! Our ultimate therapy is to surrender and rest in Christ alone, but we can find practical ways to help us every day. At different times in my life, different things were my therapy. I will list a few here.

-Long walks with fresh air and vitamin D (sunshine).
-Hot soaking baths.
-A good book.
-Holding my husband's hand on a walk through the neighborhood.
-A fire in the fireplace with my favorite beverage and some great music.
-A good long talk with a close girlfriend.

-Praise and worship.
-Spa music.

No matter the avenue for your personal therapy, you must figure what helps you rest and indulge yourself for the ultimate benefit of your marriage and your family. You simply cannot spend all of your time investing in others without investing in yourself. We are commanded to "love others as you love yourself." I found myself needing to actually take some time to love on myself and fill my cup so that I could love and pour into others. I love this quote by Andy Stanley. "You are not called to fill everybody's cup, but you are called every day to empty yours."

That is the ultimate therapy. Total surrender and letting go to let God. A daily emptying of oneself to be filled with the Holy Spirit and the associated power that comes through a yielded life. That is where our real freedom lies. That load is easier. Being led through your day by the Spirit of God is so much easier than trying to control your day. There is an inner confidence that brings flexibility when you understand His sovereignty over it all.

"I would rather live in a peace that passes all understanding than spend all my days in charge of my world and my plans."

Surrendering our pride and seeking humility and truth brings about a deep letting go. I no longer wanted to internally debate the right way of doing things. Was my father right? My husband? My children? How exhausting! I needed freedom from having to do things right. I rested in just doing the best I could. There have been many layers of revelation and learning. I would rather live in a peace that passes all understanding (Philippians 4:7) than spend all my days in charge of my world and my plans. Recognizing humility as a strength – a strength that you can gain when you walk in the freedom of truly trusting God at His word – is key. This brought me to another hungry place of seeking help and knowledge. I read the book *Humility* by Andrew Murray. I studied what the Bible teaches about humility. I was overwhelmed with the simple conclusion that humility is where the truth lies. I was born with nothing, and I will die with nothing. Everything in between is a gift from God. A gift!

When a believer chooses to surrender and trust in Jesus, the struggle does not end. It is a daily choice to surrender. It is a difficult choice in our flesh, but it is a freeing choice in the Spirit. I found it so much easier to teach Algebra and other school subjects than to teach my children that constant surrender brings a real freedom. Every day in every way I purpose to get better and better.

Being from the loud family and the right family demanded that humility be a daily choice. I failed more than I succeeded, but I was failing forward. I hungered and prayed for the truth His Word teaches. I have now come to a place where I treasure intimacy with Christ above all else – above everything the world offers. I rest in His promises. I know that my intimacy with Christ will teach our children the greatest lessons that can be taught. I wanted them to be prepared for the world ahead, but across the years, I have learned that teaching classroom subjects was a very small part of that goal.

My trust was a daily choice. His promises are always true, whether I know them or not and whether I believe them or not. I would encourage you to study His promises, to know them and to live in the freedom they can bring. Our God is a promise keeper! When all else fails, do not rely on yourself. You can and will fail yourself. He alone is trustworthy. Fix your hope on the Promise Keeper! Here are just a few of God's promises to us.

- Nothing is too difficult for Him (Genesis 18:14).

- He will work all things together for the good of those that love Him (Romans 8:28).

- He will fight for you (Deuteronomy 20:4).

- He will watch you constantly (2 Chronicles 16:9).

- He will never fail nor forsake you (Deuteronomy 31:6).

- He will give you a surpassing peace (John 14:27).

- He will supply all of your needs (Philippians 4:19).

- He will give you a hope and a future (Jeremiah 29:11).

- You will never be in need (Psalm 23:1).

- His purposes never change (Psalm 33:11).

- He will never desert you (Psalm 37:28).

- He will be faithful (Psalm 71:2).

- Everything that He has planned will happen (Isaiah 14:24).
- He will love you forever (Isaiah 55:3).

- He will defend you (1 John 2:1).

- He will listen to you (1 Peter 3:12).

- He will honor humble people (James 4:6, 10).

- He will be your friend (John 15:14-15).

- He will comfort (2 Corinthians 1:3-4).

- He has a plan for you (Ephesians 2:10)

- He will give you courage and confidence (Ephesians 3:12).

- He will complete a good work in you (Philippians 1:6).

- He will relieve you from your troubles (2 Thessalonians 1:7-8).

Some of these are general promises. Some of these are specific promises. However, the principle is that His promises are true – so is His presence and so is His power.

Prayer: *Oh Lord, thank you that your promises are always true. Thank you that your love covers a multitude of sin (1 Corinthians 13). Thank you that your love is endlessly patient, where mine is not. "I need Thee every hour …every hour I need Thee." Help me to trust and rest in you alone. Give me the strength to clothe myself in a humility that brings freedom. More of you, Lord and less of me. I trust you, Jesus!*

Chapter Twelve

What You Have IS Enough!

It is likely that we have all heard that the joy is in the journey. Well, I never have liked that statement, but I am surrendering daily to the power of accepting its truth. My original dream of our homeschool experience had many wonderful aspects to it, but it did not include growing in my own spiritual maturity. I think I envisioned things like beautiful butterflies landing on our picnic blanket as we studied science in the gorgeous backyard, which was exquisite and had no weeds, of course! I am very sure that my original dream included our perfectly dressed family all having totally obedient spirits. My children were very smart as a result of all the things that I would teach them. They were going to be Rhodes Scholars by some miraculous and divine intervention. They would be a lot smarter than the average child out there because the statistics concerning homeschooled students said so. We would do our best to be humble through our journey

"My original dream of our homeschool experience had many wonderful aspects to it, but it did not include growing in my own spiritual maturity."

since we knew all our family and neighbors would want to be like us. Our beds would be made every morning, our rooms would be clean, and our chores would be done before breakfast because we all were the early-to-bed-early-to-rise-type. We would never raise our voices and would always follow "first time obedience." I had a real picture in my head of how it would be. I couldn't wait to live inside the fulfillment of my dream.

Of course, since I was smarter than a fifth grader, I knew that we would have some hiccups along the way. I expected the Lord to teach us through those easily navigated detours. I knew about God's truth that trials build our character, so I figured there would likely be a few trials as well. My plan seemed fairly realistic in my naïve mind. I am very grateful that I didn't know what I didn't know, or I may never have started at all. He protected me. Oh, how He loves me.

The powerful truth is that the Lord knew that my deepest heart's desire was to live a life that reflected His glory. I knew that I was created ON purpose and WITH a purpose. I knew that He knit these specific children into my womb as a blessing directly from Him. I wanted children who hungered for His ways and walked daily with Him. Those dreams were not easy to chart in my daily plans. Aren't we glad that the dear Lord gives us such a deep love for our children when they are young and sweet in preparation for the time in the future when they become selfish, cantankerous, or hormonal teenagers? This must be so that we don't shoot them!

My ideas of our homeschool journey were limited by my knowledge. Since age brings wisdom, I now know that He used this process to bring about the Refiner's fire in such a way to clean out my impurities and help me become a better reflection of Him to our children. I never really dreamed that homeschooling would bring about a deeper intimacy with the Lord. My vision did not include a family closeness that was far beyond what I had known or imagined. It did not include a plan far greater than my own. I did know that Philippians 4:13 says, "I can do all things through Him who strengthens me," and I was hoping to homeschool well. But I also knew that all I had was my two fish and five loaves – my limited gifts as far as education and scholarship goes. I figured that would barely be enough, if it was even enough at all. I just trusted that God would make a way.

My original homeschool dream, however, did not include the drama and trauma, the yelling, the arguing, the missed goals, the failed classes, or the overwhelmed and exhausted teacher. It did not include a drowning mother or teenage rebellion. Where did these selfish and disrespectful growing teens come from? How could this be? Could I have failed that miserably? Wait! Wait!

Naiveté about the process might be a blessing from our dear Lord. He knows that we can only handle what we can handle. He knew my anxious heart was not yet prepared to take a drink of water from a giant fire hydrant. He instructs us to live one day at a time, for "each day has enough trouble of its own" (Matthew 6:34). If the Lord would have shown me the journey to my vision, I may never have started down the road.

I remembered the story of Joseph in the Bible. God had a much larger plan than that little shepherd boy ever dreamed possible. Thank goodness he trusted God even though he didn't understand how the vision would materialize. I wanted to trust God for my vision and my future even though I didn't know how the journey would play out.

Reading from Genesis 37, I want to relate to you my paraphrased Joseph story as we study the real Joseph story.
This is a story of how God used Joseph to save the nation of Israel. What a God-sized dream for a young shepherd boy. Roxanne felt that homeschooling four children and raising a Godly generation was a very God-sized dream as well. As the second youngest son in his family, Joseph was favored by his father, Jacob. This made his older brothers hate him. Looking back, Roxanne now feels highly favored by her Heavenly Father for having even chosen her to homeschool her children. What an unusual privilege (or nightmare, depending on the day). Joseph's brothers ridiculed him

as some of Roxanne's family and friends laughed at her, thinking she was crazy to attempt to homeschool her children. She knew there were smirks of disbelief by many naysayers.

After the Lord gave Joseph a vision of his brothers bowing down to him, they plotted to kill him. They plotted against him and said, "Here comes the dreamer! Now then, come and let us kill him and throw him into one of the pits; then let us see what will become of his dreams!" After the Lord gave Roxanne a vision of homeschooling, the enemy plotted to discourage her. After all, she was attempting a counter-cultural journey. She actually believed that she could be a fish swimming upstream against the decaying culture that the enemy was cultivating around her family. She wanted a different result for her family than what the public school might offer. The enemy hated her and said, "I will throw her into several pits and just see what becomes of her silly dreams." This was a test. Could her faith pass the test as she looked to the God who gave her the dream to begin with? Some days the pits seemed deeper than other days. Her faith was being refined.

"She didn't mind being a weirdo. Her pastor actually told her that it was okay to be 'weird' because 'normal' wasn't working."

Joseph was then stripped of the tunic he was wearing, thrown into the pit, and later sold for twenty shekels of silver. After being taken to Egypt, he was resold to Potiphar, an Egyptian officer of Pharaoh. But the Lord was with Joseph. Let me repeat: the Lord was with Joseph! Roxanne was stripped of her life of ease. She no longer was able to just simply go out to lunch with her girlfriends. Orchestrating so many daily things became very overwhelming and difficult, especially when she was walking in her own strength. Often she found herself in a pit of despair as things were not going as planned. Was it a pit created BY her, or was it a pit created FOR her? Either way, it was a pit. Often it was called discouragement, despair, and hopelessness. How could she think that she could actually rear and educate her own children "set apart as unto the Lord?" She was confused and couldn't see clearly from the pit. Maybe she should trade her dreams for an easier way. Surely they would be better off in school. Often, she felt like she lived as a weirdo in a foreign land. She didn't mind being a weirdo. Her pastor actually told her that it was okay to be "weird" because "normal" wasn't working. She felt alone in her crowded house on many days. But the Lord was with Roxanne. Let me repeat: the Lord was with Roxanne.

After becoming favored in the sight of his new master, Joseph became overseer of Pharaoh's household and all that he owned. Joseph rose to the position of Pharaoh's personal servant. Roxanne did have favor from the Lord. Many days she was able to oversee the household with an eternal vision given by the Lord to remind her that she was indeed equipped by Him to lead her children. She WAS in the center of His will. She was not the wrong mother for these kids. He had gifted her with four beautiful souls to influence, not to be a source of irritation. She needed to sit at the feet of the Lord daily in order to gather strength to manage her household. She needed to be HIS personal servant as the hands and feet of Jesus to her own children. She actually loved this job on good days. She lived her dream many days, just as Joseph was elevated in Pharaoh's household.

As the story continues, Joseph was falsely accused by Pharaoh's wife and thrown into jail. But again, the Lord was with Joseph! The Lord had a plan. It was different from the dream Joseph had seen of his brothers bowing down to him. God was working on Joseph, who needed to be refined in order to be the fruition of the very dream he had been given. As a young boy, he was not prepared to lead the nation; therefore, God allowed many things to take place that seemed to be contrary to the vision. It was not the death of a vision. It was part of the fulfillment of the vision. Joseph was lovingly inside the Refiner's fire that would purify him and allow him to be able to handle the fulfillment of the vision. Roxanne

> *"Roxanne had a plan, but God was teaching her infinitely more than she was teaching her children."*

felt unsure as to whether or not she had enough to fulfill her vision. The enemy would constantly lie to her and confuse her. She even brokenheartedly heard a child yell, "I hate you," on a particularly discouraging day. She was falsely accused by her children as being a bad mother and a bad teacher. What was worse is that she actually believed those accusations on the days that she had not spent much time with the Vision Giver. She forgot that her identity resides not in the opinions of others but in the opinion and truth of her Creator. She wanted to trust Him. Her weariness was meant to draw her near to the Giver. She needed to chill out and let go of her tight-fisted plans. He could lift her load. She felt like a failure too many days, but deep in her spirit, she knew the Vision Giver was teaching her to trust Him and His ways.

This is a story of a vision, the multiple deaths of that same vision, and then the powerful fulfillment of the vision. The only way that Joseph would ever live in the fulfillment of His vision was by the will of the Father who gave him the vision to begin with. His journey was a "becoming." Joseph just walked one day at a time, trusting the God of His vision. Roxanne had a plan, but God was teaching her infinitely more than she was teaching her children. She just didn't realize this at the time. She was trying to believe that all the screw-ups could somehow work together for good, but there were times it was hard to believe. She was learning to trust more with the dawn of every new day. There were days when Joseph may have been tempted to think, "What was I thinking that my brothers would bow down to me? I went from a pit, to being sold into slavery, to being falsely accused, and then to prison. Really?" The pathway to the vision was not expected, but neither was the mighty and powerful fulfillment of saving the nation of Israel from a famine that could have destroyed them.

Roxanne was tempted to think that same paraphrased thought. The pathway was not what she expected. It was too hard so many days. It took everything she had, and that was even not enough. The only hope for Roxanne was that she was intimately aware that her Lord could never fail or forsake her. He was, therefore, intimately present in her journey.

In my personal Joseph story, there were many deaths of the vision, days I was convinced that we would not live out the original plan to raise Godly children. Ashamedly, I let the enemy convince me that maybe I really didn't have what it took. I was simply not smart enough, not organized enough, not discipline enough, and not Godly enough. I was too much of a talker and not a good enough listener. I didn't understand why my children were not learning in the ways I wanted them to. As all four of them became teenagers, I felt so outnumbered. Not only did we miss "first time obedience," we were not obeying at all. How could this be? I had taught them to "obey their mother and their father." Wasn't that God's prescription for a long and happy life? There were L-O-N-G days and there were

U-N-H-A-P-P-Y days. Did I naively think that homeschooling could keep my children from rebelling in their teenage years? Nothing keeps our children from being sinners. At one point in those teen years, I became keenly aware that there was lying in our home. I learned that we had children making very poor choices. Illegal choices. Noooooooooo!

During this time, our family stepped out of the co-op that we had been involved in to "draw nigh unto one another" as a family. We needed to solidify our children and our family relationships. At that time, our family was pretty much grounded to only hang out with our family. We planned fun times to build family relationships that were being challenged by the world's enticements. During this time I spent most of my days either literally crying or surely crying out to the Lord. I didn't want our children to hang out with families that had children making poor choices and doing illegal things. Now we had become "that" family. We were "THEM." You know! "We don't want you to hang out with *those* people?" It was a time of humility and developing compassion.

"I was hiding behind a mask because I could not speak of such things to most people. Unlike the rest of you, I was a failure homeschool mom with rebellious kids."

170

The many facets of rebellion in our home left me totally exhausted and empty. I was hiding behind a mask because I could not speak of such things to most people. Unlike the rest of you, I was a failure homeschool mom with rebellious kids. Deep depression was knocking on my doors because I felt like such a total failure. Nobody could give me answers to my questions of "How did this happen?" or "How did we end up here?" I knew without a doubt that the enemy was totally attacking our household. We had such intentions of being HIS light to our world. Goodness gracious, we seemed to be off target.

To complicate things, all of this was happening during a season in which I was the sole caregiver of both of my parents. It was a time when their individual doctors had told me to call hospice for each of them. It was the last season of my father's life. Once, while Mom was at their senior center apartment and I was at the hospital with Dad, I received a call from a policeman, saying that he had two of my sons at the local jail. I couldn't bear to tell my father the true story, so I told him that I had to run an errand. Then I met meet Bryan to get one of the boys. We left our other son (since he was 18 years old and we could) in jail overnight as a consequence of his choices. This was certainly not our only time to deal with the police. Sadly, during that season, I got to be friends with the juvenile detention lady. I felt like we were living in a nightmare. Bryan and I were walking in dark days with barely a flashlight to lead us. We desperately needed His light in our home. I was walking such a fragile rope between my dying father, my lying children, our financial valley that required us to move, and my growing menopausal symptoms – not to mention our failing homeschool attempts. What a shock this time was to me. I had to remind myself that God was not surprised by any of this.

We prayed for wisdom daily and just loved on our children. I stopped talking so much and started praying more. I had a dear friend encourage me with "don't say it, just pray it." With defensive spirits prevailing, I could barely even discuss these heartbreaking things with the children, but I continually discussed them with God. I knew that He loved them even more than I did and that He had a plan for them. I was totally confused by what that plan might actually be at the time. I just trusted Him as I couldn't trust anyone else in our home – not even myself. *I* was even lying at times to hide much of our sin and shame. Absolutely unbelievable! I couldn't bear to speak the truth of how much sin was rampant in our home. How could I go from being a positive leader of our co-op to a discouraged hermit in such a short amount of time? It was easy to surrender all at this time as I came to believe that I had messed everything up. I was finished in every way. I was unbelievably discouraged. Deep in my soul was the spark of hope that knew without a doubt that "He can cause all things to work together for the good of those that love

Him and are called according to His plan" (Romans 8:28). I no longer wanted to have anything to do with my plan! My plan was NOT working. I cried out for mercy. I asked the sweet Lord to fulfill His promise for good as that was the only place that I could find rest. Mommas are not happy when their homes are not settled. I was not happy. Trying teenagers are hard on a marriage as well.

I believed we would settle for a different dream and just learn to like it. This made me very sad. It was never going to be satisfactory for me in the end. I was surrendering to the Dream Giver on a daily basis. I needed a lighter load. This was too difficult. Teenage rebellion, amidst our high school years, quickly dropped me to my knees. I could barely breathe at times, knowing that our home was full of lies, deceit, and poor choices.

God desires to conform us to His image. I wanted to be a pure reflection of my King. I knew that the only way gold becomes pure is to pass through the heat of the crucible in the Refiner's fire. Who likes it hot? There were times I was tempted to jump right out of that crucible. Thank goodness I had a deeper desire to be transformed by my trials than to be free of them. As I yearned to be transformed to His new creation, I discovered and realized that homeschooling was simply a process for that transformation.

I believe that each of us is created with a God-shaped void. We spend our lives trying to fill that great insatiable void with things of this world like money, toys, success, education, titles, approval, and material possessions – maybe even homeschool success. None of these things fit our God-shaped void, and none of them will bring any lasting peace or meaning to our lives. It is truly a "chasing after the wind" (Ephesians 4:6) that will never satisfy. Our only deep peace comes when we fill our God-shaped void with our creator God. The day we confess Jesus as Lord and Savior, He promises to come into our hearts and fill that previously un-fillable void. He said He would send us His Holy Spirit to fill us and comfort us. We have the power of His Spirit living within us. His Holy Spirit can help us through our most difficult days. You are an overcomer. You are an overachiever in your attempts to homeschool your children since it is NOT the easy way. But remember, you cannot embark upon this journey in a deep and satisfying way by just working in your flesh. The Lord wanted more intimacy with me, and it could only come through the trials of my homeschooling years. I now thank Him. He

"He wanted my whole heart, mind, soul, and strength in such a way as to rip everything away until there was nothing left but a sweet emptiness that demanded I lay at rest in His arms."

wanted my whole heart, mind, soul, and strength in such a way as to rip everything away until there was nothing left but a sweet emptiness that demanded I lay at rest in His arms.

I only thought that I wanted a successful homeschool journey, but eternal perspective changed what I really wanted. An eternal perspective changes how you look at everything, especially interrupted plans and what appears to be the death of your vision. I wanted to live in the sweet center of His will for my life. I wanted what He wanted for me. Through a difficult homeschool journey, He truly became the only desire of my heart. When I live my life totally surrendered, I live in a freedom that rises above it all. Desiring His will and His plan over my own plan gives me a rest that eliminates the illusion and burden of control. Often times, I felt like I lived my homeschool life in a hamster's cage, running and running. Was I getting where I wanted to go? My scholastic goals finally had to give way to relationship goals. First, I wanted an intimate relationship with my Heavenly Father that enabled me to read His Word, hear His voice, and see Him everywhere. Second, I wanted a deeply satisfying relationship with my husband. Third, I wanted successful family relationships. Last, I wanted academic success. At times, I spent more energy planning my homeschool days than I did my most important relationships.

So what is the real victory? Is it living in the purposes for which we were created? Is it a freedom and trust in Christ's plan that brings a rest that the world cannot give and does not know about? Is it making disciples of our children? Is it having a marriage and family that lives out a Christ-like example for the world to see? Is it a daily trusting of a Sovereign God? The one thing I know for sure is that the real victory comes through Christ and His ways.

I write to tell you what the enemy planned for "ill" God has now redeemed for His glory. During those fragile and hard days, I begged the Lord to show up and show off. As I totally surrendered every day in every possible way that I could think of, He started doing a great work in our home. I begged Him to bring a beauty from what looked like ashes. I trusted Him and held on to His promises (many of which are listed in Chapter 11). I consistently prayed the Lord would woo my children back to His ways. As God has redeemed and delivered us from our poor choices, we stand in awe. The ugliness and desperation took us to the cross. The Lord used the Worldview Weekend, YWAM ministries, our church and the incredible prayers of our close friends to do this redemptive and transforming work. I literally am amazed at the powerful change and the resulting family closeness that walking through those dark days has yielded. All I can say is "blessed be the name of the Lord" and "to Him be all glory." I take absolutely NO credit for His work in our children's lives. He was doing so much work on me as well.

Dearest homeschool mom:
You are affecting tomorrow by what you are doing today. Your actions will echo into the future. Your children will remember how you reacted in trying times. Trust Him! Let the Lord mold you and refashion you through the entire difficult journey. You are homeschooling the next generation. Who knows how you are impacting the world from the very confines of your own home? You are making a multi-generational impact in ways you might never live long enough to witness! Never think that you are not capable of kingdom work because you are not "enough" of something. That is a lie of the enemy. You are enough. I know about your two fish and five loaves. When you try to feed your family or others with only your two fish and five loaves, you will find yourself running empty. Your plans will fall short. It is only by releasing our plans into His greater plan that we have enough. When we give our two fish and five loaves to the Great Multiplier, not only do we have enough, but also, we have food left over. Let Him have your "little," and watch Him multiply it to being "more than enough." I am confident of this very thing, that He who began a good work in you will perfect it until the day of Christ Jesus (Philippians 1:6).

I had to remember that He alone is trustworthy (I Samuel 2:2). When I couldn't count on anything else, I knew that I could count on the fact His promises are always true (Deuteronomy 7:9). He makes beauty from ashes (Isaiah 61:3). He restores what the locusts have eaten (Joel 2:25). His mercies are new every morning (Lamentations 3:22-23). He can never fail you or forsake us (Deuteronomy 31:6). He is our strength and our shield (Psalm 28:7). He is the rock upon which we stand (Psalm 18:2) when we are so weary. We must trust Him with our faltering plans. He lavishly loves you regardless of your performance, but He desires relationship more than results. We must trust Him with our children and our marriages. Every day we must say out loud, "I trust you, Jesus." There is something about hearing our own voices speak the truth that is transforming.

"Our identity is not established in the things we own, the things we have accomplished, or in the measure of our success. Our identity is in Christ and Christ alone. In the hands of the Savior, we ARE more than enough."

Continually rest in knowing He can cause all things to work together for the good of those that love Him (Romans 8:28). He died so that you might live and live abundantly. He didn't die just so you could have a get-out-of-jail-free-card. He wants us to live with an eternal perspective and an eternal peace right here on earth. We must yield to His greater work through us;

we are His hands and feet to those in our homes and our world. Our identity is not in the things of this world. Our identity is not established in the things we own, the things we have accomplished, or in the measure of our success. Our identity is in Christ and Christ alone. In the hands of the Savior, we ARE more than enough.

Joseph ended up naming one of his two sons Manasseh, which means "God has made me forget all my trouble." Our momentary and light affliction is producing for us an eternal weight of glory far beyond comparison (2 Corinthians 4:17). Who would know that our troubles were for a far greater glory? The Lord can use our current misery for our future ministry. I want to be worthy of being entrusted with a far greater glory than my own plans.

Joseph named his other son Ephraim, which means "God made me fruitful in the land of my affliction." Is God making you fruitful in the land of your affliction? He can produce more fruit of the Spirit as we develop an intimacy with Him. He lavishly loves you regardless of your performance, but He desires relationship more than results. Don't back down from that purifying work. We are branches that will only bear fruit as we are abiding in the vine (John 15). Abide! Yield! Become! Trust! Entrust! Let Him prune you to yield more and greater fruit. It is all for His glory! All for His glory! As a result, you will live with a freedom that brings greater life and rest. Now, to Him who is able to do far more abundantly beyond all that we ask or think, according to the power that works within us, to Him be the glory (Ephesians 3:20). **He is enough!**

PRAYER: *Dearest Lord, I trust You. Teach me the ways in which I should walk, for to You I lift up my soul. Teach me to do Your will, for you are my God. Let Your good Spirit lead me on level ground. For the sake of Your name, O Lord, revive me, for I am Your servant (Psalm 143:8-12). Oh Lord, mold me and make me. You are the potter; I am the clay (Jeremiah 18:1-11). All and only for your glory. I give you everything. Multiply my fish and loaves to be MORE THAN ENOUGH!*

CONTACT ROXANNE

Do you know of a group of ladies who need some encouragement?

For questions, comments or to book a speaking engagement go to:

RoxanneParks.com

Are you being validated and encouraged in your home education journey? Do you feel overwhelmed? As a result of needing constant encouragement and inspiration throughout her homeschool journey and after 12 years of waiting for God to open the right doors, God birthed a homeschool moms' retreat in Roxanne's heart. This is accomplished through inspiring speakers, meaningful praise and worship, prayer and mentor rooms, impactful workshops and lots of joy filled laughter! The fellowship of like-minded friends and the wisdom of those who have gone before, will help you "Renew Your Vision, Refresh Your Heart and Restore Your Strength".

To register for this unique times of real encouragement, go to: www.homeschoolwintersummit.com

"The summit speakers are transparent, honest and real. Loved taking off the masks of trying to live under imagined expectations. Wow! Wow! Wow!" -Sherie

"What a surprise! This is a hidden treasure... unlike any event I have ever attended. I WILL be back every year!" –Connie

"Freedom! All I can say is freedom! You have lightened my load!" –Natalie

You are invited to experience

Homeschool Moms' Winter Summit

A Unique time of Deep Encouragement!

Renew your Vision . . .

Refresh your Heart. . .

Restore your Strength.

HOMESCHOOLWINTERSUMMIT.COM

25463860R00112

Made in the USA
Charleston, SC
31 December 2013